SUSAN WHITALL

Women of Motown:

An Oral History

DEVAULT-GRAVES
DIGITAL EDITIONS

Print Edition ISBN: 978-1-942531-26-5

Ebook ISBN: 978-1-942531-27-2

Cover design: Martina Voriskova

Title page design: Patrick Alley

Photos: All photos are courtesy of
Motown Records unless otherwise credited.

Cover photo: Cast members of Mosaic Youth Theatre
of Detroit portraying the Marvelettes in the play
"Now That I Can Dance – Motown 1962"

Layout: Patrick Alley

DEVAULT-GRAVES
DIGITAL EDITIONS
www.devault-gravesagency.com

Devault-Graves Digital Editions is an imprint of
The Devault-Graves Agency, LLC,
Memphis, Tennessee.
The names Devault-Graves Digital Editions, Lasso Books,
and Chalk Line Books are all imprints and
trademarks of The Devault-Graves Agency, LLC.
www.devault-gravesagency.com

Table of Contents

Introduction

FOR THE FIRST TEN years after Berry Gordy Jr. started
Motown in 1959, the company's history was a mystery
enclosed in an enigma, held as tightly by the company and
its roster as if they'd been working on a national defense
project, rather than making great music. But from the 1980s
on there was an explosion of ink; tell-all books about Diana
Ross and Michael Jackson, a tell-not-so-much tome by Ross
herself; various biographies and autobiographies about the
Temptations, Smokey Robinson, and Marvin Gaye. Even the
chairman himself, Gordy, finally wrote his autobiography,
To Be Loved, in 1994.

But Motown was never about one star group or one star
singer, producer, or musician. It wasn't even just about Berry
Gordy and his Motown-affiliated siblings. The two-story
house at 2648 W. Grand Blvd. in Detroit was bursting with
music, and the label's strength was its depth of talent—and a
competitive atmosphere nurtured by the paternal Gordy.

Songwriter/producers such as Norman Whitfield,
Holland-Dozier-Holland, "Brianbert" (Brian Holland and
Robert Bateman), and Smokey Robinson could take obscure

teenagers and make recording stars out of them. And the house band, the Funk Brothers, created musical textures and rhythms that helped give the records those irresistible, enduring hooks.

When I was covering music for *The Detroit News* in the 1980s, I quickly discovered that although the label had moved its headquarters to Los Angeles in 1970-'72, there were still a lot of Motown stories to cover.

One rainy day in November 1987 I was running late on my way to cover the official dedication of a state of Michigan historical marker outside the house on West Grand Boulevard. The governor of Michigan, the mayor of Detroit, Motown vice president Smokey Robinson, and assorted muckety-mucks were on hand for the ceremony, held outside, despite a sleety downpour. Several blocks around the house had been blocked off by police, but I had to get in to cover the event for a front page story. After circling the block, I flashed a press card to a police officer that declared that I was empowered to "cross all police and fire lines." This drew a round of laughter from the cops, and no parking spot. So I ended up ditching my car many blocks away and ran madly in the direction of the Motown house.

Once I made it to Hitsville's improbably hilly front lawn, my troubles weren't over. Somehow, I wasn't on the press or VIP list, so I waited out in the rain while a consultation went on. I was now beyond wet, so when a tall man standing on the porch asked if I was going to Motown's after-party at the St. Regis Hotel, I huffed, "I don't care if I ever come back here!"

"Don't say that! You're just wet!" the kindly man said. "When you come in and dry off, you'll feel better." He went in and made some noise with the powers-that-be; I vaulted over the porch railing and ventured in. I peered at my tall benefactor. "You're Marv Johnson," I said.

He was indeed. And as the singer of "Come To Me," he was truly one of the pillars of early Motown.

Marv's song "Come To Me" had been released initially on Tamla, then leased to United Artists. It became a national hit in 1959, generating money for Berry Gordy at a time when he badly needed it. Marv's follow-up, "You Got What It Takes" was another classic.

But sadly, like many early Motown stars, by the late eighties, when I met him, Marv's star had faded. He was living a spartan existence in a rented room in Detroit, left behind when the label moved west, and all but forgotten. But he still had a twinkle in his eye, and his kindness to me led to several talks. He was full of information and stories, and I meant to take them all down. I lost my chance when he died just a few years later.

I saw too many Motown greats pass on like that: artists and musicians whose talent—and hit records—initially surpassed that of labelmates such as the Supremes, but were left on the scrap heap of fame when their hits slowed down.

Whether this happened because they'd lost favor with the boss, or whether they had unrealistic expectations that the Motown family would take care of them forever, is not mine to judge.

It's a pleasure just to be able to document the story of

groups like the Marvelettes, one of the key acts in Motown's history, and too often forgotten. If I can't help Marv Johnson tell his story, at least I can preserve the stories of those I have interviewed.

The women of Motown are a particularly fascinating lot. Growing up, Berry Gordy was surrounded by many capable women, from his mother, businesswoman Bertha Gordy—a formidable force who helped mentor singer Mable John—to the four Gordy sisters: Loucye, Anna, Esther, and Gwen.

During Motown's heyday, female artists were still ghetto-ized—A&R director Mickey Stevenson admits the label couldn't release "too many" girl group records at once, because radio would only play so many—but Gordy designed Motown as the sort of place that encouraged talent, no matter the gender. The boss was as ready for female songwriters such as Janie Bradford or Sylvia Moy to hand him hit tunes as anybody.

And of course, among the most enduring images we relate to Motown are that of the girl groups, and of the classic Motown diva.

As many of us grew up, infant notions of feminine glamor were nurtured by the satiny black and white glossies of Brenda Holloway and Tammi Terrell we saw; puberty was nudged along for countless boys by the sight of Mary Wells on an album cover wearing those snug gold lamé capri pants.

The women of Motown tell their stories here roughly in the order that I believe they came into contact with Berry Gordy—the founder, chairman, and heart and soul of Motown. Some tell their story as a chronology; others, bless 'em, are more stream-of-consciousness types. I tried to preserve their voices, whatever their style.

There are sad stories to be told by and about the women of Motown, but there are many more inspiring tales, because the ones who survived are a feisty lot. I wouldn't dare take a can of hairspray from any one of them, not on your life . . .

— Susan Whitall

The Voices
[In Order of Appearance]

—*Mable John*—

Mable, the elder sister of legendary R&B singer Little Willie John, learned business skills from Berry Gordy's busy mother, Bertha. She then used that knowledge to help Gordy as an assistant as he assembled his Motown empire. As a singer, Mable benefited from Gordy's musical coaching, and she ended up performing at some of Detroit's best nightclubs. She was the first solo female to record for Motown Records.

—*Claudette Robinson*—

She was Smokey Robinson's teenage sweetheart, and later, wife. Claudette was also the sister and cousin of two of his groupmates, the late Sonny Rogers and Bobby Rogers, respectively. When Smokey tapped her to join the group, she added a sweet soprano counterpoint to the Matadors' (later, Miracles) silky vocal blend. As a young girl traveling with the Motown Revues in the South in the early sixties, she enjoyed a unique view of those turbulent times.

—Janie Bradford—

Janie Bradford was Motown's "first receptionist," but so much more, co-writing songs including "Money (That's What I Want)," and "Too Busy Thinking About My Baby," as well as dealing with artists' and writers' contracts and "mopping floors." She worked for Motown for 25 years, later starting the HAL (Heroes and Legends) Scholarship Fund, which helps struggling artists.

—Mary Wells—

The Detroit teenager wrote a song so she could meet Jackie Wilson, but ended up recording it herself for Berry Gordy. She became his first female star, thanks to Smokey Robinson's unerring sense of the songs that best suited each artist. Mary was known for her sweet disposition, innocent voice (once she stopped trying to be a blues shouter), and sometimes problematic choices in men.

—Martha Reeves—

The indefatigable Martha, stuck working as a Motown secretary, would not rest until her voice was on Motown vinyl. She sang on demos and on background well-enough that she become a top-notch Motown artist on her own, although she never could surpass Diana Ross and the Supremes' place in boss Berry Gordy's heart, leaving her with a lingering wistfulness.

—*Joyce Moore*—

The wife of R&B singer Sam Moore, of Sam & Dave fame, Joyce was associated for a time with the Rhythm and Blues Foundation, through which she met Mary Wells. She went on to work as Mary's publicist, but in fact, took on a larger role for her as medical advocate and friend in the singer's vulnerable last years.

—*Kim Weston*—

The native Detroiter graduated from Miller High School, and was singing with the gospel group The Wright Special by the late 1950s. Brought to Motown in 1961, she signed a contract and "Love All The Way" was her first single. She recorded memorably on her own and with Marvin Gaye, and was married to Mickey Stevenson, Motown's first A&R chief. The two left the label and both signed with MGM Records. In recent years, Kim worked in arts programs for the city of Detroit.

—*Mickey Stevenson*—

Stevenson was the fast-talking, very east side (of Detroit) guy Berry Gordy relished for his street wisdom and his invigorating presence in the Motown boardroom as the company's A&R director. His job was not only to find and sign talent to Motown, but to shepherd them through the recording process. He also produced records for the Marvelettes, Martha Reeves, the Velvelettes, and Kim Weston. He married Kim in the early sixties.

—Brenda Holloway—

The sultry Los Angeles teen dreamed of being a Motown singer while she was mopping her kitchen floor, listening to Mary Wells on the radio. She became one of the label's more polished female singers, and considered herself a favorite of Berry Gordy's, although being half a continent away from Detroit meant she missed out on the better songs.

—Katherine Anderson Schaffner—

A girl from suburban Inkster with a talent for singing, Katherine and her fellow Marvelettes competed in their Inkster High School talent show, which led to an audition at Motown. "Please, Mr. Postman" was the song they brought to Detroit, hoping the company would like it—and them.

—Carolyn "Cal" Gill Street—

Although she was the youngest Velvelette, Kalamazoo native Cal had the feistiness and drive so key to a lead singer's success. With the overnight success of "Needle In A Haystack," she went to live with an aunt and uncle in Detroit and transferred to a high school there, where she signed autographs for fans in the school hallway.

—Norma Barbee Fairhurst—

The Flint girl joined her cousin Bertha in a family singing group, the Barbees. When Bertha formed a girl group at Western Michigan University in the early sixties, Norma was called in again to lend her soprano to the smooth mix that became the Velvelettes.

—Lynda Laurence—

Lynda was the Philadelphia-born daughter of Ira Tucker, lead singer for the Dixie Hummingbirds, and by the time she was tapped to replace Cindy Birdsong in the Supremes she was already a smooth, showbiz professional.

—Scherrie Payne—

Scherrie grew up in Detroit, the younger sister to Freda Payne ("Band Of Gold"). She admired the Supremes from afar, and ditched her job teaching school to sing full-time for her boyfriend Lamont Dozier's record company. It seemed an impossible dream, but she did eventually become a Supreme.

—Mildred Gill Arbor—

A student at Western Michigan University with a knack for singing, Millie was swept into the Velvelettes; she brought her little sister Cal over from Loy Norrix High School and gave them their lead singer. Millie never gave up her day job; she earned a degree in nursing and for years worked the night shift.

—Bertha Barbee McNeal—

The ringleader of the Velvelettes, the Flint native was an aspiring teacher when she gathered a bunch of girls together in a practice room at Western Michigan University in Kalamazoo, and with the addition of a few ringers, managed to create a Motown-ready girl group.

—Tammi Terrell—

As Tammi Montgomery, the outgoing, flirty Philadelphian already had a long career behind her as a singer, having performed with James Brown and other stars before she came to Detroit and formed an immortal singing partnership with Marvin Gaye.

—Elaine Jesmer—

Jesmer is a former Motown publicist who worked closely with Tammi Terrell, Marvin Gaye, and other of the label's artists. She is the author of the long out-of-print Motown roman a clef, *Number One With A Bullet.*

Chapter One
—Mable John—

MABLE JOHN IS THE *oldest sibling in the Detroit clan that produced legendary R&B singer Little Willie John, the incendiary performer whose brief career produced such genre-defining classics as "Fever" (covered later by Peggy Lee).*

Big sister Mable belongs in the music record books on her own; she was the first female Berry Gordy signed as a solo artist—to Tamla, his start-up label. But she toiled hitless at the hometown company until she left in 1964; it wasn't until her stint at Stax Records in Memphis that she scored a hit in 1966, with "Your Good Thing (Is About To End)."

In the fifties John toured with her brother Willie, one of the major R&B attractions of the day. In 1969 she went on the road with Ray Charles, as the lead Raelette. She quit Charles' show one day in 1977, when she says she heard God tell her, "Go home!" The mother of four did, and she became a practicing minister and pastor of her own church in Los Angeles. She also heads up the Joy Community Outreach To End Homelessness charity.

When Mable John visits Detroit in the wintertime,

you're likely to see her swathed in fur, a slight but command-
ing presence.

There is about her, still, the sleekness of Detroit's
silk-stocking nightclub era, a hint of the glamorous singer
who played the Flame Showbar back when girl singers were
expected to exude class and sophistication, as well as put
over a hot tune.

—Mable John—

I was born in Bastrop, Louisiana. Nobody's ever heard
of Bastrop, it's so small. And then my mother, father, and I
moved to Arkansas. That's where all of my sisters and brothers
were born except two, my two youngest brothers, who were
born in Detroit. There are six brothers, and two sisters, under
me. Three girls and six boys, and I'm the oldest. Willie [Little
Willie John] was the fifth child.

My father worked at a mill where they made paper, in
Arkansas. In Louisiana he worked on what they called a log
pond, where when they cut the trees, they would put them
into a little pond, and they would roll the logs to the other
side, to the mill, where they'd go through some kind of
conveyor where they'd cut all the bark off the trees, and get
the wood ready to make paper. Which is quite interesting in
itself, to know how paper is made.

When they moved from Louisiana to Arkansas, my
father worked at the paper mill, a larger firm, then a few years
later, 1941, we moved from Arkansas to Detroit. My father

had heard, when we were in Arkansas, that the automobile factories were open, and he could make more money. He and some friends drove from Arkansas to Detroit. We stayed behind until he arrived and was able to get a job, and he found a house. And I guess it was maybe six months before we followed behind.

We lived at Six Mile and Dequindre Road. At that time there was a project, where the property had been loaned to the city by Henry Ford, and we moved in there, they were brand new (originally built as temporary housing for World War II factory workers). We were all children at that time. I attended Cleveland Intermediate School, and then Pershing High School, which is at Seven Mile and Ryan Road. On Dequindre near Davison was the elementary school some of my brothers and sisters attended.

The whole family—Johns and Robinsons alike—was musical.

On both my mother's and my father's side, they loved to play guitars and the piano, and sing. And they did it basically for fun. I had great uncles and cousins in Louisiana who had horses, and they would ride, especially on Saturdays and Sundays, from one farm to the other. All the way they were singing and playing guitar. And of course my mother's mother was a Methodist lady, and she was always cooking and raising funds somehow for the church, for some mission or women's auxiliary.

She would have Friday night fish fries, and my uncles

made homemade whisky, and the people would drink and sing. My mother learned to play guitar, and my father did, because it was on both sides of my background. They never sang professionally, but when we were little children, just able to walk around, that's what my mother and father would have us do, sing for fun. They'd work in the fields all week, and on the weekend they ate fish, they drank, and they sang.

My mother never drank, but my father did. He was so talented that he could watch anyone do anything and then he would come home, get my mother's pots and pans, and make every instrumental sound that he had heard. And he could sing the song. He was very, very talented.

Mable met the formidable matriarch, Bertha Gordy, before she met Berry.

I met his mother when I was a teenager, and I hadn't finished high school. Mrs. Gordy was one of the founders of Friendship Mutual Insurance Agency, and she would come through the neighborhood knocking on doors and selling insurance. At that time, people would do that. My father never liked talking about insurance, because to him it was making preparations to die, and it put a little fear in him. So when she would stop at our house, they would just be involved in general conversation, because she knew she could not talk to him about insurance.

1959 at the Flame Showbar, Detroit. L-R, Robert Gordy (Berry's brother),
Billie Holiday, Berry Gordy Jr., Mable John, and unidentified friend.
(Courtesy of Mable John)

I wanted a job after school when I went into high school.
My father never wanted me to work. But he agreed that Mrs.
Gordy could take me into the office and train me. So I started
working in her company after school and on the weekends, so
that she could give me some clerical experience. Meanwhile,
I became so interested in selling and the way that they would
train people to sell the insurance that I asked her to please let
me sell the insurance. So she would carry me with her.

Later on, after I finished school and I spent two years at
Lewis Business College, I kind of lost track of the insurance
company. It later merged with Supreme Liberty Life Insurance
Company. [When] I ran into Mrs. Gordy again, I was grown.

She wanted to know what I was doing, and she started telling me that her son Berry was writing songs. He hadn't had anything recorded, he did not have a company, but he was writing songs and he was trying to get different people to record them. And the person that he knew most of all was [singer and Highland Park native] Jackie Wilson.

So Mrs. Gordy said to me, if you come over to my home one afternoon, I will introduce you to him. I told her I was coaching choirs at my church, and I was the state musical minister; they had five churches in the state of Michigan, and I was going from church to church. One was in Pontiac, one in Flint, one in Inkster, and two in Detroit. So she said, "Well, if you're doing all of that, why don't you let my son work with you, and you could make some money singing, because you're doing this just for free."

So I went over to their home on St. Antoine and Farnsworth, and met Berry. And of course at that time he was just getting started; Detroit was not even on the map hardly. My brother [Little Willie John] had begun to sing and travel, and he and Sugar Chile Robinson [a Detroit nine-year-old who scored a number four national R&B hit, "Numbers Boogie," in 1949], they were the only people from Detroit who had made any history musically for Detroit.

Rhythm and blues had not had any claim hardly, and there were no black labels at the time; there weren't really a lot of black disc jockeys at the radio stations. There were a few, but not a lot. My brother was signed to King Records, and that's where a lot of the black singers were, at King, because the people at King were blues. At that time they weren't even calling it rhythm and blues, when Willie and Sugar Chile started. They named it that later when we were getting more black deejays, and when Berry Gordy got more deeply into it.

[Berry] started out as a writer and a coach for new artists. When he began working with me, he only had the Miracles, who had not recorded. A lot of us, we went a few years without a record company. Because he would write the songs, he would coach us, he would play piano for us. When I played my first engagement, he played the piano for me! He played for years until he just decided that he was a crutch for me, and if I was going to make it, I'd need to be comfortable with other musicians.

The last time he played for me was the last show Billie Holiday did, in Detroit [in 1959, at the upscale Flame Showbar], just two or three weeks before she passed away. He put me on that show with her. And Maurice King was the conductor.

Aside from being coached by him, John also worked with Gordy as a sort of de facto assistant. It helped that she had a car.

I was with Berry Gordy when the black disc jockeys' organization was organized. They used to hold their meetings at a little club on the east side called Lee's Sensation.

There at Lee's Sensation, right in the back room, all the black disc jockeys would hold their meetings, and Berry Gordy and I would be there. Because Berry didn't drive at that time, and didn't have a car—I don't know if Berry drives now! He might, I don't know. Later on, down the years, he had enough money to hire a driver. But I would drive him. A guy I was dating, I would use his car, because I had his car all the time, and wherever Berry had to go, I was the one doing the driving.

I made the sandwiches and the punch to serve at the meetings at Lee's Sensation, to serve after the meeting. That's how I got to know them. We wanted to be sure that all of the disc jockeys would play the music that Berry was writing for the black artists to sing. That's when black music really came into being, when the black jocks were able to land jobs at the different radio stations.

Black disc jockeys from all over the United States came. They'd come from Kentucky, St. Louis, Chicago, Philadelphia, Florida, Tennessee. The one thing that helped black music a lot, and the music that Berry was writing, was a guy named John R. [John Richbourg], out of Nashville, Tennessee. They used to call them hillbilly stations; I can't think of the call letters [WLAC]. John R. played black music like mad, he mixed it in with the country music. We could depend on, if we listened to him, hearing our records played. In fact, he's the one who broke all my records through the South.

And he was not black, but he became a part of the black music scene because he loved that music. That was when the music classification changed; because before then, they called it race music. And it wasn't played fluently on white stations because it was race music. A few were, but not like it happened from 1956, '57 and on, and up to now. So when that organization was formed, it gave Berry a platform to express what he wanted to do, and the black disc jockey organization decided that they were going to make him a household word and play the music.

At that time Berry organized his publishing company, and I would drive him to the airport almost every Friday. He'd fly to New York and he would spend the day peddling or hustling his music. He would go from record company to record company all day long on Fridays, playing his music, auditioning his artists to other companies, like Sepia, Mercury, Atlantic, Brunswick—because most of your record companies at that time were based in New York.

Mable John in her hitmaking Stax Records years.
(Courtesy of Mable John)

And basically what he was able to do, because of Jackie Wilson being from Detroit, and him knowing Nat Tarnapol, who was the manager of Jackie Wilson, he was able to get Jackie Wilson to record his songs and they became hits. So when Jackie became a hit, that put Berry on the map. So he was able to get awards, BMI Awards, for the songs, because some of them went gold.

In those years Berry did not like to do interviews. He's older now, more experienced, he has more to talk about. But then, he was talking about what his hopes and dreams were, and now he can talk about what he did. But back then, I would do the interviews instead of him. I would go to the radio stations to promote the records. That was before he even released anything on me.

Before Tamla, before Motown, Berry Gordy was in the business of coaching, writing songs for, and producing artists such as Mable John and brokering their services to record companies.

First he signed me to United Artists, and they never released a thing on me. We were at a BMI function in New York, just before Jackie Wilson—I don't know if it was before someone stabbed Jackie, or before he was shot—I think he was stabbed before he was shot. Anyway, Jackie was there because Berry was getting an award. I had gone to work at the Apollo Theater with my brother, and we closed at the Apollo the same week the BMI Awards were in New York. Berry called me and asked me to remain there, since they were all coming in from Detroit because he was getting an award for one of the Jackie Wilson songs he had written.

You might see a photograph, in the museum or in books, with me, Berry Gordy, Ray [Singleton Gordy, Berry's second wife], Berry's mother and father, and Jackie Wilson. That's the picture that was made that night in New York, at that awards dinner. That must have been 1960 or '61. That night, sitting at the table at that awards banquet, Smokey Robinson and I told Berry Gordy that he should start his own record company, and I said to Berry, "If you start your own company, I'll record for you, and I'll stay with you forever."

His words back to me were, "Don't ever promise anyone that you'll stay with them forever. What if I can't give you what you're looking for, and you find somebody who can? If you want to move forward, you would have to go where you could get what you're looking for. But we'll always be friends and family."

And that has remained true. And that was the beginning of him thinking about starting a company of his own, because I don't think that was his original idea.

Gordy said he wanted to start his own label so he'd be able to keep more of the money his songs were generating.

I don't know if Berry had a money problem, but we all had a money problem! And I'm sure he had problems getting his money, because number one, at that time none of us knew the business. Not any of us.

But what Berry's family did was the same thing that my

family did. The whole family of both of us came together, because we were accustomed to working together as a family. We decided, if we were going to venture into this, that the family was going to get involved, so that's what the Gordy family did, and the John family did also. And we all learned the business. And that was the thing that actually strengthened both sides, both of our families.

Because at one time Berry's family gave him money. Because when you start out, brand new, you don't really know how much it's going to cost you to do what you have to do. And you can go bankrupt, literally and actually, trying to do it, because you're learning as you're doing. While you're learning, you're finding out that you need X amount of dollars to stay afloat. If you do have a tight-knit family, the family can get together and fund you, and cushion you until you're able to go to the next plateau.

That's what the Johns did, we all started writing songs, traveling and working with each other, and that's the thing that strengthened us, and we were able to grow.

Although Gordy and Mable John were close, her brother Little Willie John never had a professional relationship with Motown.

Willie started first, and he was becoming successful very fast. He and Berry would talk, but there was always this little thing with my brother. He would become a little jealous sometimes because I spent so much time with Berry. Actually, I think that's one of the reasons it was so easy for my brother to take me on the road with him, because he thought he was taking me away from Berry. He would always tell me, "I'd like you to go with me and do so-and-so." I'd say, "No I have to do this with Berry." Then he'd say, "But I'm your brother."

They admired each other. But since Willie started first and became famous first, because he went directly to a major label [King, in Cincinnati], they didn't really work together. But I think, in both of their hearts, they would have loved to have done something together.

When Berry put me in the Flame Showbar with Billie Holiday, Willie was living with his wife in Philadelphia at the time. He flew in so he could be with me on closing night. That was the highlight of that week, along with working with Billie Holiday.

Billie Holiday was awesome, and she gave me a lot of nuggets that I've lived and built my career on. Because I didn't have the success with record sales as other artists at Motown, but I think that I was a trailblazer, and I laid the groundwork for a lot of things that went on. Being more administrative and business-minded, and learning the business.

She would sit and talk to me. And because she was so heavily into the narcotics scene, she would let me know that was a route that I should take a detour from. And she would say things like, "You have to know when you've done enough of anything, and you have to have guts enough to stop, on your own." She said nobody will ever tell you when you've done enough, not if it's beneficial to them. They'll keep pushing you to keep going, keep doing more. But you'll know when you've done enough.

All kinds of things she'd say, maybe not speaking directly, or naming individuals, but she let me know that she went too far, that she had been pushed too far, and when people keep pushing and pulling you, all of a sudden you're at the point of no return. She'd tell me to learn from other people's experiences. You have to learn to become a people watcher.

I learned contracts and learned how to tear them apart, see what was best for me in the contract—not being selfish, I know that anyone who gives me a contract, it has to be beneficial to them too. But I had to look for the benefit for both sides; she would tell me about that. And it really helped me.

Another thing that Berry would do, every big name that would come to town—Dakota Staton, Della Reese, Sarah Vaughan, Dinah Washington—he would take me to the Flame Showbar and sit me there at a table, and I would sit at least two nights, because the shows ran seven nights. At least two of the nights, he would have me watch them perform; not the men, but the women performers.

He said, "These ladies have already made it, these are great ladies. Watch these ladies." Then he would have me critique them. Then he put me with [Flame Showbar bandleader] Maurice King, and he had him start coaching and grooming me. And Maurice King had me to come back all over again, just to watch Dakota Staton. He said, "I want you to watch how she walks onstage. I want you to watch how she backs away from the mic at the end of her song. I want you to watch how she takes a bow, I want you to watch how she uses her hands. You watch her, because she's very classy."

Dakota traveled with George Shearing at the piano. I

learned so much from her. Then he had me come back, to watch Dinah Washington. He said, "Now I want you to watch how she comes on, how she talks when she's on, and watch her whole demeanor."

Then he'd say, "Of the two singers, which one would you prefer patterning your mannerisms by?" I said, "Well, I'd love to be able to sing like Dinah Washington, and have the poise and the class of Dakota Staton." He said, "Well then, remember both ladies, and correct yourself by it." Those were the kind of things that I did in the early years.

I was with Berry for four or five years before I ever recorded, because I started with him in the fifties, and my first release was in '61. So it was four years. In '56 he started coaching me. In '59 I started recording, but my first release was "Who Would Love A Man Like That?" Berry wrote it and produced it on me.

I was the first female solo artist signed, and that was not to Motown, that was to Tamla, the first label he organized. Motown came later. The Miracles were also on Tamla. Claudette [Robinson] was with the Miracles, but she was not signed as a female artist, she was signed as part of that group. So I was the absolute first.

Mable's music is a refreshing reminder of how funky and bluesy Gordy liked his music in the early days.

The company started out that way. Listen to the [pre-Motown] Jackie Wilson songs, those first songs [Gordy wrote]. Listen to the early, early years of Stevie Wonder. Listen to early Mary Wells. That's the way it started off. And he knew, and he coached me for blues. And listen to Marv Johnson. All of those in the first, beginning years were blues, because that's what blacks sang.

But there came a point when John could see that Gordy and Motown were firmly on a mainstream, pop path that wasn't quite right for her.

It was the artists that came, and the airplay that was received, and the crossover market. When the white jocks would start to play the black music, which I don't believe there's no such thing, by the way, as "black" music. Music is music; it can be jazz, blues, rock, and to prove it, everybody's singing everything now, every race. So it's no longer race music, it's just music. But when the white stations began to play our music, then they'd say, "She's gone pop." It was the same song! But then you had other artists who weren't quite as bluesy, and it made it easier to program them on all the stations.

I don't know if it was Berry's idea, or it evolved to that. I don't know what his idea was, because the way he wrote— and you see, he brought in other writers who wrote different ways. The Holland brothers wrote differently, Mickey Stevenson, Clarence Paul, Janie Bradford, they were writing straight across the board. And when you have people writing songs a certain way, when they hear a certain person with a certain kind of voice, they'd say, "That song is good for so-and-so." And when they would learn the song, and the song's becoming a hit, and everybody's playing it, you just kind of go the way the success is going. I think that's basically what happened.

After then we started getting knowledge about different categories of music. When you find you have a winner, you stick with the winner. You should! Most of my success came from Stax Records, where they did concentrate on more soulful-sounding music. I fell right in the pocket there, because that's my pocket! Later on, when I got with Ray Charles, and traveling with my brother Willie, I learned other songs. But they still have my same flavor because that's me.

I went to Stax in 1966. Motown was just turning so pop, and I knew I wasn't pop, but the writers were writing for success. The success that the company was starting to enjoy was from the pop scene. So they geared all their writing to the ones who had actually gone pop. Berry was so busy with the business, and I found myself without a writer to concentrate on me as Berry had concentrated on me.

Clarence Paul did some things on me, Holland and Dozier did some things on me, Mickey Stevenson did several things with me, but all in all, my element was getting lost. And it was Lucky Cordell in Chicago—he was in Gary, Indiana at first, then he moved to WVON in Chicago. And he said there was a new label, like a year later, it was opening up in Memphis, and it was a soul label. Al Bell, whom I had met in Nashville years ago, was there kind of spearheading it. So Lucky said, "I'm going to send your Tamla releases to them and see if I can work a deal for you." And he did. And Al Bell flew into Chicago.

They had never met me, they didn't have one thing written for me when I got there. I sat down, and Isaac Hayes played the piano, and I would start telling them stories. And David Porter would begin to formulate the words that I was saying on paper, to make them fall with the music that Isaac was playing. And that's where my biggest hit came from, "Your Good Thing's (About To Come To An End)."

It came from that particular union, in 1966. But Berry and I remained friends, and we still are.

Chapter Two
—*Claudette Robinson*—

MABLE JOHN MAY HAVE been the first solo female artist signed to a Berry Gordy-owned label, and Mary Wells was clearly Motown's first female star, but step back. Claudette Robinson claims for herself the title of "First Lady of Motown," because she was the first female artist signed to a Motown-related label—as a member of the Miracles.

Robinson is a gregarious raconteur, gracious toward her ex-husband, Smokey Robinson, and philosophical about the ups and downs of her career as a singer. As she tells her stories, there is often a mischievous arch of the eyebrow or twinkle in her eye that lets you know she's no plaster saint.

Smokey's future muse was born in New Orleans and moved to Detroit with her family when she was eight years old. Claudette Rogers lived on the city's east side from the age of eleven until she married William "Smokey" Robinson in 1958. Smokey was eighteen when they married, and according to most estimates, Claudette was three years younger, although she won't comment directly about her age. (Internet sources have her born in 1942, two years after Smokey).

She met Smokey through her brother Sonny, who was in the Matadors, an early incarnation of the Miracles. Her cousin Bobby Rogers also became a member of the group. When Sonny was drafted into the Army, the Matadors needed another voice, so a smitten Smokey decided Claudette should join. And it made for a good mix: her voice was on top, Smokey sang lead, Bobby Rogers' tenor was under Claudette, then came Ronnie White's baritone and Pete Moore's bass on the bottom.

Berry Gordy decided the band needed a less masculine name if it was going to include a female member, so they became The Miracles, and Gordy managed and recorded them for several years before he started up Tamla Records. The Miracles were the first band Gordy signed. The group also scored Motown's first million-selling single, "Shop Around."

It would seem that the early years of their marriage would have been difficult for the Robinsons, with their constant touring, a serious illness of Smokey's, and the heartbreak of Claudette's numerous miscarriages. But she remembers those years as the most intense fun of her life, full of what she calls "the joy of being young."

Theirs was considered one of the closest marriages in the Motown stable, and if anything, the Robinsons' union seemed to strengthen through the years, as they struggled to have a family. The gorgeous ballad "More Love," with its line "more love, more joy, than age or time could ever destroy," was Smokey's most famous public declaration to Claudette.

So when Smokey and Claudette divorced in 1986, it was

*a shock to many. Smokey had become involved with another
woman, who bore his child. He and Claudette have had their
ups and downs, but have maintained a cordial relationship,
as the parents of Berry William, born in 1968, and Tamla
Claudette, born in 1969.*

*When I spoke to Claudette in the spring of '97, she and
Smokey were preparing to become grandparents for the first
time. Their daughter Tamla gave birth to a daughter on July
19, 1997. Grandpa Smokey named the baby Lyric Claudette.*

—Claudette Robinson—

In the formative years of my life, I was living in the South
with my grandmother. She was the secretary of the church.
Her brother, my great-uncle, was the pastor of the church,
so as far back as I can remember, I was always singing in the
church. My earliest recollection of singing was when I was
three years old, when I sang in front of the National Baptist
Convention in Monroe, Louisiana. And even though I've
always been kind of shy, and in my latter years, reserved, it's
hard for me to imagine I could have been standing up in front
of all those people doing anything.

When I was in Catholic school, the nuns would always
be trying to get me to sing something. When I was older,
they wanted to take me to New York to get some training.
Of course, my grandmother wouldn't allow that, but I had
no desire to become a professional singer. I always enjoyed
singing, and music, but I never thought I had the personality

for show business. I thought you had to be outgoing, real aggressive, and actually that's not true at all. In fact most people in the industry are shy.

I went to the High School of Commerce in Detroit. I studied college prep and commercial business. The High School of Commerce was next door to Cass Tech. You would take your college prep classes over at Cass Tech. Then we learned how to type, how to do bookkeeping, how to operate the calculator, [and] how to use the mimeograph machine at the High School of Commerce.

I graduated when I was fifteen. I was a fast typist, so I worked at the downtown YMCA for fifty cents an hour. When I was in college they gave me a permanent job. I went to Wayne State and Highland Park Junior College. I thought, this was wonderful, a full-time job, having your own office. I accepted without thinking that my mother was going to kill me because she wanted me to keep on in school. I promised her that I'd go on, in night school. And I did, for a while.

I met Smokey when he was fourteen. My brother Sonny introduced me; he was a member of the group before they were the Miracles. The Miracles only began when I became part of the group and we recorded our first single. Their group was called the Matadors, and I had a sister group called the Matadorettes. I always had a group whenever my brother had one. He had a group called the Orchids; I had one called the Orchidettes.

I loved to sing, I love to sing today, and I love to hear people sing, and I love performing, but I just never even had the slightest clue that one day the music that we were singing would still be recognized almost forty years later. For me, I couldn't begin to imagine that that was even a possibility. Because it was difficult to even get your records played on the air. There were only a few black stations, and that's where you always had to be played, first and foremost.

Smokey has been very blessed to have been given the talent of a voice, and the ability to write fantastic lyrics. I think that it's a gift because I don't think it's something that can be taught to you. You either have it or you don't. Lots of people write songs, great songs, but if you really look at it, you'd be thinking, well what are they saying? They may start off talking about the weather, then finding a girlfriend, then they end up buying a car. Poor example, but many times the songs don't seem to make much sense.

But when I look back, I think of Smokey being so young and writing songs about love that actually he could not have had the experience to know about. You know what I mean? How many people had he been with? You just have to experience it, "it" being love, before you really know about it. When you're very young you think, I'm in love, I know all about this stuff.

Claudette didn't fall for skinny young Bill Robinson right away, although he was smitten with her, by his own account.

That's what they tell me. I was only a kid! It wasn't like I was trying to be in love with people. Just a little girl!

Claudette Robinson and the guys. Left to right:
Bobby Rogers, Ron White, Smokey Robinson, Marv Tarplin, Pete Moore.
(Courtesy of Claudette Robinson)

We didn't go to the same high school. I graduated before he did because I graduated at fifteen. We didn't even live in the same neighborhood. Our meeting was just happenstance. Of course, there was my brother meeting up with them. Actually my brother [Sonny] met Pete [Moore] first; they were both going to Cass Tech. My brother—he passed away several years ago—was very talented musically, given the gift of a voice. He was real good with harmony. Basically he could take the voice, he could take each person, and without a piano or anything, give them a note and give them perfect harmony.

He used to always say that I was the one with the better voice, but I was very shy. I don't think I used that talent to the fullest.

The only way I could have run into Smokey was through my brother. There wouldn't have been any other way. He went to Northern High School, he lived on the north end, and I lived on the east side. Unless he happened to come to my church or dances, skating, or bowling, I don't think we ever would have met. And if we would've met that way, I'm not sure I would have paid any attention to him.

When I did meet him, I didn't look at him and say, "Oh, God, he is really cute." When I was younger, you know how you choose the looks of guys you think you're going to be with? Well, he wasn't it. But he was a nice guy, one of the nicest guys I'd ever met. And he's still a nice guy, he truly is. Even though we've gone through our divorce, we can still laugh and talk. We're about to be grandparents! Smokey's getting his own set of bedroom furniture for the baby, I'm getting mine, and my daughter's getting hers. It's going to be too much.

Despite Claudette's show of indifference, Smokey was starting to get under her skin. The Matadors rehearsed constantly at the Rogers house, and Claudette and her friends would spy on them.

I remember they were rehearsing in the basement of my house, these five guys, and it was very hot, and there were a lot of girls who lived on my particular block, so we were looking down at the guys, looking through the basement window. And Smokey took his shirt off. Well, Smokey was six feet tall and weighed probably about 135, so all these ribs were showing! So when he took his shirt off, the other girls started laughing. I'd liked him as a person, but I wasn't thinking about liking him as a boyfriend. At that point I really and truly started liking him, because I was so sad for him, that they were laughing at him. It was like, here comes the underdog. I'll take care of him.

And we started talking. I suppose he had been talking to me all along, but I hadn't paid much attention. When you're young, boys would be saying things to you, but I couldn't even imagine how they could like me, because I was still trying to develop; long legs, very thin. A lot of the girls were very developed; they had the whole thing; breasts, hips, legs. Me, I didn't have any of that. I was the little girl.

And yet Smokey once said that the teenaged Claudette had the best body of any woman in the world.

Claudette Robinson in the early 1960s.
(Courtesy of Claudette Robinson)

You know what? I've heard that he said that, but it's hard for me to imagine. I had a very tiny waistline, and I had hips, but they were covered up, so I don't know how anybody knew that. I remember once, the first time that I met Jackie Wilson, I remember him walking behind me and going *"Oooooo!"* And I was, mind you, very shy. So I wanted to cover my eyes up; I was so embarrassed. I didn't think of "this body" or anything. It's like a lot of things that escape you over the years. I wasn't into the physical, how a person looked.

When I was growing up I liked tall guys, more dark-complected, but they didn't have to have a certain nose or eye color. I looked at the person, what's inside, not outside. And I'm glad for that. I think my mom gave me that insight for people. It's what's on the inside that counts, not how tall or how anything. It's the person in that person. She'd always say the eyes are the mirror of a person's soul. She'd say look in the person's eyes, because if you're looking away from people, they don't know if you're listening, if you're the kind of person to be deceitful.

I have a wonderful mom, Viola Rogers, the finest lady in the universe. She lives in Detroit and we don't see each other enough, but we talk a lot, often every day. She was a little strict, but she says had she not been that way, then I would not have turned out to be the lady that I am. I can't tell you what happened or why or how, but something prevented me from doing things. They just were not on my mind. That's not to put me on another plane, that I'm this wonderful, perfect person. I didn't want to get into trouble, so I avoided it at all costs. I wasn't the rebellious type; I conformed to society.

I think, as soon as I hit the stage and they said "The Miracles!" and I took that one deep breath, any nervousness I felt at that point kind of left, until I went back offstage. Because you have a job to perform like any other. You really have to practice, just like electronics or plumbing. Practice, try to improve and do better. With a group you have to do routines, your harmony, even the way your hands would go, together rather than one person going one way, and the other another way. So it's timing, and precision, and trying to get it right.

There's a lot of preparation that goes into getting onstage before you're actually there. In fact we learned that very quickly after our first professional date. We did five weeks, all the major theaters at that time that had shows: the Apollo in New York, the Howard in Washington, the Royal in Baltimore, the Regal in Chicago, and the Uptown in Philadelphia.

On our very first date, at the Apollo, we had our routine we had planned, but we were young and inexperienced. We didn't have television like you do today, where you could watch other acts and see what they were doing. At that time groups were jumping offstage, doing splits offstage, jumping up, almost doing acrobatics.

And we had our nice little routine where we went three from stage right and two from stage left, and we joined each other in the center; the music stopped, and we clapped for the next eighteen bars. And that was it, that was our routine! That was really a lot of time wasted, but that was our plan. At that time Motown really hadn't started, even though we were with Berry. So ours was a true learning experience.

In his book **To Be Loved,** *Berry Gordy related a story about an early Miracles concert at the Apollo when Smokey was so nervous, and the crowd so contemptuous, that he supposedly tried to dance in a fruitless attempt to entertain.*

Oh, Smokey was not the dancer of the group. I mean, he can dance, he has rhythm; his timing was OK. He can slow-dance very well . . . but he tightens up onstage. He's a lot freer offstage, as far as dancing goes. But performing is really his life; he actually loves to entertain and perform for people. And he's been doing it for many years. They say he was singing before he could even walk, when he was in his walker moving around.

I loved it, but I wasn't thinking of it as my lifetime career. I was thinking of it as something we'd do for a few years, then we'd get back to real life, and go on to whatever you do after that, family and jobs, nine to five. Because at that time artists, especially black artists, didn't make a lot of money from performing. So it was very difficult to see how you were going to make a living and make enough to support a family. We were kids and had no children or anything, we didn't have a house to maintain, so it's a lot easier when you don't. You can just float around when it's just two people.

Sheltered as she was, being in a band including her husband and brother, Claudette didn't have any security worries on the road.

I was protected on the road! I had the best experience of anybody, being on the road. Because having all these guys around, there was no way I had to worry about other guys. When we were on the road, no one had a clue as to who was with who. Most of the people on the road, especially the girls, thought Smokey was my brother.

I remember a particular group, I shall leave them nameless. Smokey would always go and ask if I could share a dressing room with the girls, because they only give us one dressing room. And all I was going to do in there was dress, because even though I was a part of the group, and was "one of the guys," I wasn't a guy, and I wasn't going to dress or undress in front of them.

So he would ask if I could share their room, and they were gracious, they said yes. And I went into this dressing room, and they were just talking on and on about how *niiiiice* this guy Smokey was, and then they said, "That's your brother, right?" 'cause they'd asked what was my last name. I said, "No, he's my husband." They'd say, "Your husband? How old are you?" I'd say, "I'm old enough to be married."

Smokey was nineteen when we were married. I never say how old I am. I was in the vicinity of . . . whatever. At that time we thought we were just so mature and grown-up. I look at our wedding picture occasionally and I'm amazed.

Although the racial climate in the South in the early sixties was still volatile, Claudette remembers more good times than bad.

I want to tell what it was like on the road. Sometimes you hear such horror stories. It was not horrible—if it was, we would not have stayed out there. Of course there were circumstances; sometimes when prejudice exists, it's very blatant, other times it wouldn't be obvious.

On the road, I would call for reservations for the next place we were going because we were usually traveling by car, and it would take into the next day before we would get there. And I would make reservations for, usually, four rooms. And we'd get to the place and pull up, and somebody would get out, or we'd all get out, and we'd say, "We have reservations for tonight," and give our names. And they'd say, "Ohhh . . . we're all booked up."

I would probably speak up and say, "Booked up? Well, that's not so, because I just called"—ten hours, or eight hours ago, sometimes not even that long. And they were all set for us to come there. Well, if we stayed around too long, in some places, I must tell you, we knew to get out of there, because sometimes the people would come from the back with a rifle or something.

It was difficult finding a place to stay, which is why in the early years many of the artists stayed in rooming houses; somebody had a house and they'd kind of convert it. That was the only place you could stay. Even as far as places to eat, you couldn't go everywhere. Not only just sitting down, you couldn't even order at some of the places. They just wouldn't allow it.

If you were going to order something, you'd have to go around to the back, and as far as using restrooms, there was only one restroom for blacks; men or women, they'd have to use the same one because there was no distinction.

With the separate water fountains and all that, it was really something. It wasn't that long ago. I remember someone saying when he was a little guy, and the water fountain said "colored," and "white," he couldn't wait to get over to the colored water fountain because he thought the water was going to be colored! He thought he was going to see blue or green or pink water.

Motown worked the Miracles, sending them out on several grueling Motown Revues, which were station wagon and bus tours with few stops for food or rest. Youth carried them a good way, but Smokey was always susceptible to respiratory complaints. One time Claudette had to step forward and impersonate "Smokey" on the Motown Revue after he'd gone home sick.

Smokey had come down with the first case that they knew of, or we knew of anyway, of Asian flu. Hong Kong flu is what they called it at that time. He had a fever of 106. And nobody really knew what was wrong with him. They were saying they didn't have a bed for him, and they had to pack him in ice to get that temperature down. And at the hospital they had him really out in the hallway because they didn't have a bed for him, and if they had a bed, it was only a bed for charity patients.

Mind you, we were almost a charity case! This was in the early days; it wasn't like we had a lot of money! *[laughs]* We should have just said yes, give us the bed because we need it! So he had to go back home, back to Detroit. So I took him back home, and his niece Sylvia was going to take care of him. Sylvia was about a year older than Smokey, but they grew up like sister and brother. He was home for about a month. I went back on the road, and I filled in.

Back then it wasn't like instant television, where you just click on, or the Internet where you can instantly see photos of people. If you had never gone to a group's city, and you had never seen them perform before live, the chances were, especially in the early years, you didn't know what they looked like.

And so as a result, you heard the high voice, and when they saw the girl, they just assumed that I was "Smokey." So I was singing his songs, the ones that he did lead on, and they were yelling like, "Ooooh, Smokey! Smokey!" *[laughs]* But it was a time when we all really had to pitch in, because not only was our lead singer out ill, and was going to be for a month, our bass singer wasn't there. He was in the United States Army; he'd been drafted. So we had three people: myself, Bobby [Rogers], and Ronnie [White]! So it was difficult, but we got through it. And we were headlining the show, needless to say. Mary Wells was the co-headliner. And she had polyps on her throat . . . wasn't that something!

To make things even more complicated, while she was out singing as "Smokey," Claudette found that she was pregnant.

I got pregnant—I mean, I *was* pregnant, and when I discovered that I was, I was in pretty bad shape. I did not have one of those pregnancies where you are all peaches and cream. I was just sick, sick, sick. I was so sick I couldn't keep one morsel of food down. Unfortunately that pregnancy, as well as many others, ended in miscarriage. After I discovered it and could finally come home, that was the pregnancy I carried for six months. Most of the others were six, six and a half months. It was not easy, but youth . . . you know that statement that youth is wasted on the young? If you could have that kind of feeling when you're older, which I try to recapture now and then, what a wonderful way to live, if you could ever do that.

Because you're so freed up, you're innocent, you don't really have the baggage that you may have later on in life, you're just . . . free. Full of life and ready to live and go for it. Especially in terms of the miscarriages, the doctors would say, "Well, you're very young, and next time . . ." Pretty soon, it was like, I'm not going to be young forever. At the time, when they'd say "next time," they'd try to tell me what had gone wrong, although they really didn't know. They didn't have the medical technology that they have today, and as a result, they were not able to do the things that they can do today.

There was some thought that the endless touring was a strain on Claudette. Smokey eventually asked her to give up going out on the road.

I don't think it was being on the road so much, because

54

I had miscarriages after I came off the road. So I'm not going to say that it did or didn't, I'm not sure. Smokey felt that my health was suffering, which I suppose anybody would probably feel. I think it was a condition, and I'm blessed to have any children.

Claudette toured with the Miracles until the early '60s, and recorded with them until 1965. Her voice is on most of their biggest hits, and yet with a star as magnetic and talented as Smokey Robinson, it's almost inevitable that her contributions, and those of the rest of the group, have been underrated. On the **Motown Master Series Smokey Robinson & The Miracles Anthology,** *there are only a few group photos that include Claudette.*

My biggest thing is that I really want the world to know that the Miracles—and Smokey is a Miracle—were the very first group, with Berry, with Motown, and that I was the first female. Berry gave me the title of First Lady of Motown. For the longest time, it was very difficult to say that because you didn't want people to think you were tooting your own horn, patting yourself on the back. It wasn't that, but history needs to be corrected, and for people to know two hundred years from now how the story of Motown really began.

Because there are people who think the Four Tops started it, the Temptations; some people think it was the Supremes. The thing is, even when you're reading the books, you're never really sure. It's confusing if you don't really know.

In his autobiography To Be Loved, *Berry Gordy claimed that it was Claudette's voice on the first version of "Shop Around."*

I've read that, and I've heard that I cut a version of "Shop Around." I don't remember that. Smokey basically always did the lead. There were times I may have done a demo for him. But as far as for release . . . What might be confusing is that if someone got an old tape, in the early years, sometimes when we recorded certain songs, it was difficult for people to know if it was me singing or if it was Smokey, because his voice was so high.

In his last year of high school, Smokey sang with the soprano section. So he had a very high voice. I was listening to something the other day that wasn't released . . . we did an album called *The Miracles Sing Modern*. I had about two tunes that I sang lead on, and I ran across it the other day, and I turned it on, and someone was at my house, and they were humming along, and they said, "Who was that? Is that you Claudette? I never knew you guys sang songs like that."

What happened was, we were preparing for a nightclub act, which we did, although we didn't do a lot of clubs, but we worked with Cholly Atkins, and he had us gliding across the floor, doing all kinds of things; we got all dressed up in our little clothes. I have a few photographs onstage, doing these clubs, and [in] one photograph of us, we're singing "Summertime," and we have these fans in our hands. Pete is the one leading the song; he's our bass singer.

I didn't have a difficult time knowing which was which between Smokey and myself; I could tell, but I could understand other people not being able to tell quite as well. Because you just hear two high voices and you're just assuming that they're both mine.

Claudette was married to the writer of some of the most romantic songs in the world. She doesn't hesitate to name the Smokey Robinson song with the most personal meaning for her.

"More Love." 'Cause that's the only one I felt that he wrote specifically for me.

Berry Gordy wrote in To Be Loved *that he had no idea Claudette and Smokey were romantically involved. He also noted that her looks helped interest him in the group, and that in fact, he called Claudette up at one point for a date.*

Again, youth. When he called me, I really didn't know that that's what he was calling me about. To me, I hate to use this term, but to me he was an older gentleman . . . an older guy. He was very much a gentleman about it. He called; I was part of the group, and he had all our numbers, and he said, "Claudette, this is Berry Gordy." And of course I gave him respect, as you did to your elders. I know he'll kill me if he hears me say that. I said, "Yes?" He said, "How are you doing?" I said, "Fine." He said, "Do you have a boyfriend?" I said,

"Yes." He said, "Do you love him?" I said, "Yes." And he said, "What's his name?" I said, "Smokey." He said, "Oh, OK, that's good . . . I'll talk to you later." I didn't know he was hitting on me, I just thought he wanted information.

But I found out later because he told me the story later. He said, "Shoot, you were cute." You know, that's the strangest thing, I never thought I was cute. My brother used to say— and I discovered so much later, it took me a trillion years, that when brothers say things, they're just saying something. But I thought he was saying the truth. Because I loved him, he loved me, and how could he be telling me something if it wasn't true? My brother told me that I had a nose like a pig.

Honestly, we were laughing about that just before he died. In the last week of his life, I came back to Michigan, not knowing that he was going to be gone; I kept waiting for him to get better. So we had a lot of conversations about our childhood, and what he did. I told him, "I used to wonder what I could do to my nose, because you kept telling me I had a nose like a pig." He said, "Oh sister, you didn't really believe that, did you?" I said, "Yeah, because why wouldn't you be telling me that, if it wasn't true?" Then Smokey told me that my brother used to tell all his friends, "Man, I have a *fiiiine* sister." Well. . . too late! It's even funny to me when guys will come, who knew me when I was growing up, and they say, "God, I used to love you when you were whatever age."

And I say, "Well, you never said anything to me! And they say, "Well, we didn't know if we could!"

And I thought hmm, whatever.

After a long marriage, and such a public breakup, Claudette is serene and friendly with her ex-husband.

Oh, it was hard during the divorce. You know, divorce is a tearing apart. This is my analogy: first you're two people, when you get married you come together as one. When you're divorced you have to now become two again. And that's that tearing apart, that's your heartstrings you've torn out, your whole life. It's your life, it's your companion, it's your lover, it's your friend, it's so many things that this person is to you and for you and with you, and all of a sudden . . . I was probably more shocked than some of the people around.

It also was difficult because of other people. The concentration was not what Claudette is feeling now, and what she's dealing with. They were trying to trying to figure out how we could get back together. And that's all they would be talking to me about. "This is just a phase, you guys are going to be back together."

Even today, I must tell you . . . I have gone to concerts in Las Vegas, and Smokey almost always introduces me from the stage. So people come over and talk to me, and they're saying, "We're praying for you, we just know that you'll get together." I suppose this is because we're both still single. Probably if one of us had married or something, maybe they would have, by now, gotten over it or something. When they see us together, I think they think we're back together, too.

I'll say "no." I even overheard a conversation once, people were discussing, you know how people are behind you and don't know you're there? One said, "You know, I thought

Smokey and his wife were separated." And the other one said, "No, I think they got a divorce." And the other one was saying, "Well, they must have gotten back together, because I saw them at such-and-such, and they were walking around together holding hands."

And it's like, when you know somebody that long . . . sure, it was really hard. I can't tell you it was an easy task. But years have passed now, and time is a healer. If you were talking to me eight or ten years ago, I probably would have a different conversation with you in terms of him, or whatever.

I was very, very hurt. I was heartbroken. I had just a number of things you have to deal with and go through, and yet he was constantly, continuing to tell me how much he loved me. It was hard for me to compute that through my brain. I think it sometimes made it more difficult, because it wasn't a clean break, where people move on and you can get over it, or deal with it in an easier manner. I think even people who want a divorce, both parties, while they're going through it, end up having a bad time. Divorce is never pleasant, from either side. He was the one who filed for it, but he, too, did not have an easy time of it.

Smokey and Claudette embodied romantic love for many fans, because of all those Miracles and Smokey Robinson love songs. "Ooo Baby Baby," "More Love," "You've Really Got A Hold On Me," etc.

I, too, felt that way. With people initially, if they really love each other and care for each other, you think it's going to be forever. But I think the circumstances, especially with the onset of him having this other child, in some ways he thought that he would be protecting me. That may not make a lot of sense to you, but so that he didn't want me to have to go through what he felt was the hurt and the pain of what people would be saying, how they'd react to me. I wasn't sure either, how to handle that or what to do with that.

Because whatever a person is doing, you may not know what they're doing, but once a child exists, then you know. Whether it was one time or a million, it doesn't matter. The fact of the matter is, this is something that comes and disrupts our lives, meaning mine, his, and the children's. Because divorce is not something that just affects the two people who are married.

Nobody wins in divorce, the children first of all, and friends, family. It's a lose-lose situation all the way around. Unless it's people who just got married for reasons or conditions, or what they could get from it. For us, there was nothing either of us had, except for each other *[laughs]*. Smokey made $5 a week. So, I certainly didn't marry him for his money. He got a raise to eight dollars!

And yes I still have faith in marriage, and yes, I still think there are good men around, and yes, I still believe that there are people who are monogamous in their relationships, and sometimes, yes, I do look at the world through rose-colored glasses. I see bright hope, and I'm still dreaming, and I'm in love with love, I'm a romanticist at heart and by nature. I love to be in love, I love being romanced, all of the things that go with that, the flowers and the hearts and butterflies.

It's phenomenal to me to realize that people are enjoying the music today, as they were when it was first released. It's amazing. I don't know if I can really express it. I'm extremely grateful and proud that people can still enjoy it, and I feel very blessed that through all of this time, the "Sound of Young America" is still young. Practically forty years later, it's still young music; young people can relate, and older people— several generations.

Seeing the Motown Museum, in connection with the one at Greenfield Village [at the Henry Ford Museum], I was pleasantly surprised and kind of in awe, because then you can remember.

A lot of things don't stay in your mind, stories behind the scene and all that, but then looking at the pictures on the walls, looking at the tapes running in the little theatre at the Henry Ford Museum, I think, gosh, we really did a lot of things.

Chapter Three
—Janie Bradford—

LIKE MANY OF HER *Motown colleagues, Janie Bradford was the daughter of a minister, a Detroiter with roots in the South.*

Janie was a student at Cass Tech High School, a Detroit magnet school that drew the cream of the city's youth (Miss Diane Ross was also a Cass Tech girl), when her interest in poetry was piqued by a poet's visit to one of her classes.

Once she was hired at Motown, like many, she had a job title—"first receptionist"—that didn't quite reflect her true status. She also wrote songs—which is how she first met Berry Gordy, as a teenager—and she co-wrote several notable ones, including "Money (That's What I Want)" with Barrett Strong and the boss, that are among Motown's finest.

Janie moved to Los Angeles in 1972. She retired from Motown in the eighties. In the ensuing years, she launched the Janie Bradford HAL Scholarship Fund (with its annual Heroes and Legends fundraiser), published the entertainment magazine Music Connection, *and ran songwriting workshops.*

She returned to Detroit in the spring of 1997 to record

a Christmas song, "The Present," with an all-star group of Motown artists. I was having breakfast with her in an Eastern Market cafe when "More Love" happened to come over the sound system. "There's always Smokey," Janie said with a laugh. "You sit anywhere in the world, in ten minutes you're going to hear Smokey."

—Janie Bradford—

I used to write poems when I was in high school, at Cass Tech, and put them on the bulletin board. When I met Mr. Gordy, I told him I could write songs. I could not. I'd never written a song. But I was just as tall then as I am now. And you know how kids are—I was pretty self-confident.

Janie forgot about the encounter. But Gordy didn't. He needed songs, so he came looking for the statuesque, cocky teenager.

He was looking for a song, so he came by my house, since we'd exchanged addresses and phone numbers. He wanted to hear my songs, or look at my lyrics or whatever, and suddenly it hit me. I just invited him in, and went and got my book of poetry, and I played it off like I thought they were song lyrics. He taught me how to take the poetry out and put the lyrical movement in, and the hook—tell the story and all this kind of stuff.

From that first meeting, in not too much time, I had two

songs out on the Jackie Wilson *Lonely Teardrops* album. One is "The Joke's Not On Me," and the other is a ballad. I can't think of the name of it to save me.

How did a teenager happen to meet Berry Gordy?

Jackie was the one that introduced us to Berry. I'd met Jackie through my sister; she's a singer. They worked together, and he invited her down to check out his show. I wanted to go, but they kept saying, "You're not old enough." But Jackie had said, "I want to introduce you to my writer." See, Jackie was not a celebrity in my eyes. You know how if you know somebody, then they're not a celebrity? But this songwriter [Berry Gordy], he was the celebrity. And so I couldn't wait to meet this songwriter. I had to plead and beg 'til they finally let me go, and that's when I met him.

I don't know what I was expecting, but Mr. Gordy was just a human man, flesh and blood. I was disappointed because there was no halo and no wings.

I was only fourteen, and you know how when you're fourteen, you're brash. I blurted out, "You can't write any songs. I can write songs better than you can, any day." So that's how he thought I really had some songs. Which I did not, until all of it came together.

Gordy wrote "Reet Petite" and "Lonely Teardrops" for Wilson, among other numbers, which helped him launch Motown.

I don't think he ever really got paid, but it did give him the start, and the contacts, and the entrée into the business.

Janie wrote songs with Gordy during his pre-Motown days. Later, when he started up his own record company, there was no specific job offer. Janie was simply "there."

At Motown, I did everything. In the beginning, I was there from day one, there was no first job. You can say I was the receptionist. They had a receptionist desk reserved for me, and it said "Janie Bradford, first receptionist," which I was, but at that time I also did the artists' contracts, I did the writers' contracts, mopped the floor. You did whatever had to be done.

The most famous song Janie Bradford's name is attached to has to be "Money (That's What I Want)," recorded by Barrett Strong (and later, the Beatles).

Mr. Gordy was doing a riff on the piano, and he was just really getting into the rhythm, the pattern of the song. He said, "I need a title, give me a title, something that everybody wants." I said, "Money, that's what I want!" So that's how he and I came to collaborate on that. We often did things like that in that day. We would all just hang around, and whoever was there would just come together and work. You'd get a workable hook. Repetition was the key, get a title that would work and relate to just about everybody.

I want to say it's not one of my proudest works—it is,

financially—but I have other things that I think are lyrically so perfect, so beautiful, but they're on an album, so nothing ever happened to them. One of my favorites was a tune Carolyn Crawford did, I wrote it with Smokey, "My Smile Is Just A Frown Turned Upside Down." I thought that was pretty unique. It kind of hit and missed the charts, it never really peaked. But from that song we got a cult following for the last thirty or thirty-five years. Everybody overseas knows about that song and Carolyn Crawford, but it did nothing here.

Janie credits Gordy for being a boss who expected excellence from both his male and female staffers.

Berry was supportive of creativity. If he sees talent or something that can be developed in a person, he can reach out and tag that person and work with them and develop that talent.

There weren't that many other opportunities for women back then. Mr. Gordy molded me, just like every writer who came through in the beginning. It was almost like a class. He'd praise you, he'd say, "This is good, but it could be better if you did this." His thing was, "Why settle for gold, when you could have platinum? Yes it's a good song, but if you did this, it could be even greater." He'd work a lot with the writers in the beginning. But after the second year, you were kind of on your own.

Janie found herself wanting to help other songwriters who pitched songs at Motown.

My desk was next to whoever was listening to the songs and accepting them or rejecting them. Most of them were rejected. And some of the ones I'd hear, I'd think, they could have saved that song. If he only had told the writer, "if you'd done the title different, if you'd repeated your hook more, or if you'd changed the melody." I'd think, when I'm in a position to do this . . . then I thought, wait a minute, I *am* in a position to do this. So about twenty years ago I started a songwriters' workshop, for a very minimal fee, to help writers and let them grow. From that I've started a HAL (Heroes and Legends) Scholarship Fund, to help students with limited funds.

Janie was one of the Motown staffers invited along to California when the company moved, in a lengthy process, from 1970-'72.

We were always out there, back and forth, and I loved California, so I just packed my bags.

Her long sojourn at Motown came to an end in the early eighties, but Janie doesn't hold any grudges.

Everybody got good severance pay if they were there for any length of time. It wasn't compulsory, but it was done. That's how I was able to start my other businesses. That stuff is never told. That company was such a blessing to us, a bunch of kids with no direction, going nowhere, given somewhere to grow.

I think everybody thinks because Mr. Gordy invested his

money that everybody who walked through those doors, he's still supposed to support them. And half of them just blew their money. The company gets a lot of bad rap because of that. Personally, I think there were a lot of things wrong, like there is with many companies, but there was so much more that was right. And the opportunities! Like I said, I didn't even know what a song was. It was really an open door, a blessing for us. People always want more. I do too, if I can get it! When did "Money" come out, thirty-five, forty years ago? And the checks are still coming in the mailbox. I'd probably be getting ready to retire from Ford [Motor Company] or somewhere, had it not been for that.

The Gordys were a hard-working family. There's been no company like Motown, the whole thing, to make the artist a total person, not just send them out there when they can't even speak.

In the beginning, a lot of the writers used to complain because if you had $10,000 coming, the finance department would only give us eight and hold back two. Because they knew you were going to be broke, so rather than you coming back to borrow money, you'd be coming back for your own money.

Your nickname at Motown was "Brick House."

Time eradicates everything.

Chapter Four
—Mary Wells—

YOU NEED LOOK NO further than the career of Mary Wells to see the physical manifestation of the shift at Motown from bluesy, gutbucket music to the sweeter pop that would put the company on the charts and into the black. Her ascent also revealed the importance of Smokey Robinson in creating the Motown sound, because it was Robinson who steered her away from the funky wail Gordy was encouraging in early Wells songs like "Come To Me" and "I Don't Want To Take A Chance." Robinson encouraged Wells to sound sweet and shy, closer to her personality than the blues mama Gordy had in mind.

Her voice had the perfect, girlish sound for such sensitive Robinson compositions as "The One Who Really Loves You," "You Beat Me To The Punch," "Two Lovers," and of course, "My Guy."

She was born in Detroit in 1943. As a teenager, Wells helped her mother clean office buildings in downtown Detroit. She was just shy of graduating from Northwestern High School when she met Berry Gordy, Jr., and her life changed forever. Mary Wells was seventeen when she signed with Motown. She soon became the top female star Gordy had longed for. Although her career and personal life deteriorated tremendously in the twenty years after she left Motown, it was still a shockingly premature death when Wells died of lung cancer on July 26, 1992, at the age of forty-nine.

—Martha Reeves—

Mary Wells was the first Motown star. Mable John was more of a friend to Berry, and her brother [Little Willie John] was in the business, so she sort of helped Berry learn the publishing business. She was good on the executive side, for him. Mary approached Berry at a record hop, where he was working with Marv Johnson, I think, or Barrett Strong. [Berry] had one of those artists out on the circuit—that sort of thing doesn't exist anymore.

And Mary approached him and said, "I have a song," and she sang it for him. He said, "No, you've got to cut this yourself," and made her an artist. He took very good care of her. He was like a father figure to her. So she was his first discovery. Mable John may be the first signed to Motown, but Mary was the first Motown female that Berry discovered and signed.

Joyce Moore was a friend and publicist in Mary's later years, just prior to the singer's death.

—Joyce Moore—

Mary wrote this song, "Bye Bye Baby," because she had
a terrible crush on Jackie Wilson. She wrote it for Jackie, and
took it to Berry, who at that point was songwriting for Jackie.
Berry had her come in to demo it, and when he heard her do
it he said, "No, it's not for Jackie, it's for you." And that's how
the relationship started. She was a teenager.

Not many people know that Mary and Jackie once went
together. She went with him later, after Jackie was going with
and then married to Harlean. '65, '66, '67, somewhere in
there. Mary and Jackie were very, very close to each other, had
had an affair, relationship, whatever you want to call it. Later
Mary also had a relationship with Carl Davis, Jackie's producer.
In fact, when Mary went to Atlantic, Carl produced "Dear
Lover," which was Mary's big hit at Atlantic. A very substantial
hit. Carl and Mary were engaged.

Carl was absolutely, drop-dead in love with her, bought
her an engagement ring.

—Mable John—

I knew Mary when she first came to Motown, when she
was a teenager that everyone was running wild over. Mary
Wells was, to me, one of the nicest girls that walked in there.
She was like a kid. And we would literally almost have to hide
her, to get her from the car to where we were performing,
because the children would tear her apart! And of course we

shared one recording session together, when I did the song "No Love," and she did "Bye Bye Baby." Berry took a group of us to New York to a studio, to record us there. At that time there were not a lot of great studios in Detroit, so he took the Miracles, myself, and Mary Wells, and we laid our vocal tracks there.

We were very good friends.

—Mickey Stevenson—

The first record I did on Mary was "I Don't Want To Take A Chance," I think. Her innocence was her greatest strength. Mary Wells had a very innocent sound, almost a childlike innocence. It wasn't a great voice, but it was such an innocent voice, you were drawn into her sincerity. She had not been tainted.

We made it a point to try to protect all our artists, because they were young, and their youth and inexperience didn't help them dealing with and living the life outside. As they got involved in outside things, especially in Mary's case, her choices were not the best ones, as a young woman. Which is a very hard thing for most females in our business, the business of entertainment. They're more susceptible to relationships that are not beneficial to what they're about, and where they're going, I think. This is my personal opinion.

The question has always been whether or not Mary really did sign away the rights to her royalties.

We did everything we could to try to protect Mary. I personally was involved in trying to protect Mary because I knew of her innocent approach to everything. But her husband [Herman Griffin] had ideas of his own, and since he was in control of her future, he took care of all of that. He made all those things that were not good for her happiness. It was not Mary's fault. She was following the line of her husband, who had aspirations of his own. He wanted to be a big entrepreneur in the music industry.

Here's a guy who would go onstage and conduct her music. Who could not read or write! And since he was her husband, and she wanted him to do whatever he wanted to do, we had to go along with it.

In the middle of a ballad, he'd do a backover flip like Jackie Wilson! At the Apollo Theater! You get the picture? You can imagine how I felt, I'm carrying out the Motown Revue, I'm controlling the entire Revue, and I've got to stand by and watch this guy do these things. I'm from Detroit too, so I come from a different mold; I could have stopped him. But Berry said no, none of that, this is all about business. But he's killing this girl!

I was not very happy about that at all. But Berry was very calm, he said, "Legally, that's her husband, she wanted him to conduct." I said, "Yeah, but this is our company!" He said, "Yeah, but if we don't let him, he'll only be trouble for you later on in other things."

So he had to put on his mohair striped suit, know what I'm saying? He's ready. Powder and makeup on, he was ready to go out and conduct the orchestra. And do a backover flip, in the middle of a ballad! The audience at the Apollo was like, *"Whaaaat?"* He was a frustrated performer.

When he didn't want Mary to perform, he would make it difficult. Then he'd step on my toes, and I would do something about it. My job was to see that everybody cut their albums, did their product, and he got to the point where if he didn't like something else, he wouldn't have her come in. So I would have to go and get her.

In 1964, Wells tried to renegotiate the contract she'd signed at seventeen, but couldn't come to terms with Gordy, so she left Motown at twenty-one. Next she signed with 20th Century-Fox Records, then Atlantic/Atco, Jubilee, Reprise, and Epic. She had her biggest post-Motown success at Atco, although nothing ever matched the magic Smokey Robinson was able to elicit from her. In 1966, she married Cecil Womack (brother of Bobby). They had three children: Cecil Jr., Stacey, and Harry.

—Mable John—

I wasn't surprised [when Mary left Motown]. I was able to understand clearly. See, some people are put in the world to start you off, as a beginner, to give you your foundation. It doesn't mean that this is the place you're going to end up. It has to do with what's going on in the individual's heart, what are you looking for? You can see certain things in me, but that might not be what I'm trying to attain. I might be trying for something much different. But you must start there.

But I believe that when your foundation is right—and Motown was the best foundation that anybody ever had—if you could have been there in the beginning to see what the plan was, the plan was for each artist to be an artist, not a gimmick. Those were Berry's words. He said he didn't need a gimmick; they could use some comedy person for that. He said he wasn't looking for comedy; he was looking for artists. Because if you're a good artist you don't even need a record to work, once you became established. He wanted to build musical artists, not just recording artists, and that's what he did.

And you know, many of the original Motown artists don't have recording contracts at this time. But they work, because number one, the way he groomed the artists, they could work anywhere and anytime. And that is the greatest foundation you can have.

—*Martha Reeves*—

Mary was very proud of her position as Berry's first female star. She showed a little jealousy when we talked over the fact that other people came and just moved her right out of the spot, but she didn't understand the system. I got it, eventually.

They would make you, then move on to the next artist. Mary was different than most of us because she wrote some of her songs. We weren't writers. I was a writer, but I didn't want to write. I found that there wasn't much of an advantage to being a writer at Motown. But she wrote many of her songs and had that ability. Her first album after Motown was very good. She just didn't get the promotion that she needed. But she continued, and some of her songs could have hit if she had the right promotion. When she left the company, Berry assigned her royalties to someone else. Did I ever tell you that? For all these years that people were looking at Berry, saying he was rotten and low down, when she and her husband took her from Motown, they signed with some other people, and [signed a contract release that let Motown] out of [paying] her royalties. That was her ticket to get out of Motown. So he didn't owe her anything. The people who were getting those royalties, no telling what they did with the money, but her daughters certainly don't benefit from it. Her children, she has three, don't benefit. They live in Los Angeles.

I was very close with Mary. I did all of her last engagements the last year she was alive. And I did see her getting weaker and sicker and weaker and sicker and closer to death. She didn't stop smoking. I guess she'd gotten too far and just wouldn't stop.

—*Joyce Moore*—

Mary put too much [faith] in Berry Gordy. Berry Gordy and her first husband were the first two guys who [messed her over] royally. And when she wouldn't capitulate to Berry—look at Diana Ross and Mary; Diana would probably kill me for saying this, but there's a strong resemblance between those two.

From what I understand from Mary, she wanted to be released, when she realized that the million dollars or better that the company made off "My Guy" and her hits went into Diana Ross, who Berry by that time was having a relationship with. If you make a million dollars off somebody, put some of it back into that person, at least. That's what pissed Mary off. Mary went in asking to renegotiate, in order to be free and released from her contract, which was for slave wages. The first money Berry Gordy really made was from Mary Wells.

—Brenda Holloway—

My boyfriend right now, Jerome, I met him in '91 when he organized a tribute day for Mary Wells and Brenda Holloway. Mary was the real recipient, though, because she was sick. And we got a chance to sit down and talk and know each other for one day, a complete day. And she told me, "Brenda, I wish we'd known each other before." She was telling me that she had some regrets, and she would have lived her life a bit differently, and more spiritually. At that point I took my watch off, my beautiful, beautiful watch that I loved, and I said "Mary, please wear this." And I gave it to her, and she was buried in that watch. But I got a chance to meet the real Mary.

Because there was a facade around her. She was very unhappy. The men in her life were bad choices, and she let them guide her in the wrong direction all the time. It was a wrong mix. But she was a beautiful, sensitive person, and she had many regrets that she shared. And I fell in love with her. In the sixties, it was like "Oh, she's an untouchable." Because she was the one with all the hits! We were wannabes, we were trying to be her. Everything she touched, when she was with Smokey, turned to gold. So she was Miss Motown.

—Katherine Anderson Schaffner—

Mary was a very sweet young lady. I think all of us were very naive to the business and the hangers-on that became a part of your life. But Mary was a very sweet girl, a very talented lady, because Mary did help to write many of her own songs.

I wasn't surprised that she didn't do as well away from Motown. Personal opinion is, if you left Motown, that was like leaving the godfather. And I didn't see where the interest, number one, would necessarily be there with another company. But it almost appeared as though you were blackballed, because by then Motown and upper management were very strong and very powerful. Many of the artists who have left through the years, none of them have done very well, especially those who started, grassroots, with Motown.

The only artist I can remember who came to Motown and then left and went into a better position contractually would be Gladys Knight and the Pips, when they left Motown for Buddah. But I haven't seen any other artists who have done that.

I don't know if Mary necessarily signed away her royalties so much as they were manipulated away from her. Because things that she'd written, of course, she should have received a writer's royalty. But nobody was around who would advise you to your own benefit. So you had to look to the powers-that-be to guide you in the right way. We didn't have show business attorneys in the Detroit area, as we know them now. Many of the attorneys could read over your contract; however, they couldn't make any changes because they weren't familiar with show business contracts.

Therefore, I would say Mary was jilted out of what was justifiably hers. It's all right to share the wealth, but it becomes greed when you take it. That's what happened with Mary. It also happened with me, on a song I wrote. Gladys Knight's "I Don't Want To Do Wrong." But when it came time that it was recorded, my contract ended up being something like two percent. Well, how the hell do you get two percent out of 100?

So I think that she was more or less jilted out of [her royalties], because they more or less gave her minimal percentage and took the larger part for themselves. And anything that you wrote for Motown became Motown's property, of course, because they made it part of their [Jobete Music] catalog.

—Carolyn "Cal" Gill Street—

We [the Velvelettes] worked with Mary Wells, we did gigs with her, traveled with her. We worked with her in Saginaw, Michigan a couple years before she passed away.

She may not have had the savvy or the knowledge to market herself in a way that would be beneficial to her. And she may not have had the powers-that-be behind her and pushing her. There might have been some sort of sabotage preventing her success, who knows. I don't know exactly what Mary's problem was, but some forces were working against her, and I think that even though there are those among us who are chosen to be leaders and to be successful, there's still no guarantee that we're going to be that way if we don't take advantage of everything put in front of us.

—Norma Barbee Fairhurst—

We [the Velvelettes] performed together [in the late eighties]: Junior Walker, the Contours, Mary Wells, the Velvelettes. She visited with us in our dressing room, and she was sitting there in a haze. I said, "Mary, what's the matter?" She said, "I just admire you ladies very much." "Why?" I said. "You never left the industry." [She said,] "Because you were able to leave the industry, for years and years [the Velvelettes all married, had day jobs, and let the group slide at times before reuniting]. And then to come back, as if you'd never left." I could still see the beauty there, the features . . . she looked a little weary, but we all look that way when you're mothering and have a lot of responsibilities.

In the seventies and eighties Wells made her living on the thriving oldies circuit, where she would sweep out onstage coiffed in the long blond wigs and sequined sheaths expected of Motown's first diva. But backstage, her life was unraveling. Her marriage to Cecil Womack ended in divorce, and she was going with his brother, Curtis Womack. She had a baby, Sugar, by Curtis, and was still playing the oldies circuit in the late eighties, when she met Joyce Moore of the Rhythm & Blues Foundation. Moore was married to Sam Moore of the sixties soul act Sam & Dave, and would become friend, press representative, and health care advocate for Wells in her last few years of life.

—Joyce Moore—

Sam was out on the road, we would be out on some oldies packages together, which is how I first met Mary. I didn't know her during the height of her career. I knew her in the later part of her career when she was . . . a mess.

She was, I later found out, and was told by her, a heroin addict who intermittently used methadone and did other drugs. She had Sugar out on the road with her; of course, she had just had her. I don't remember being around Mary pre-Sugar. We didn't start doing oldies packages with her until fairly late on [in the late eighties], and Sugar was an infant. I remember her taking a bassinet and putting it near the stage, and having Sugar there while she'd go out and do a show. She had Curtis with her, who was her live-in lover, but they were never married.

She'd been married to Curtis's brother Cecil, and had three children from that relationship. Sugar was Curtis' child. So she had four Womack children. Curtis and Mary's relationship seemed to be loving, but tremendously dysfunctional. Curtis was very devoted to the baby and reasonably devoted to Mary, but just totally dysfunctional. They always looked dirty, they never looked put together, although when Mary went out onstage, you'd never know it. But in her personal life, she was unkempt.

It was from the drug addiction. There were times on the road, there was one date in Fort Hood, Texas, I ended up driving them from Austin, Texas to Fort Hood, then back again. And they were nice enough, but I also know that they had no money with them, and until they got paid they couldn't afford to eat, and they were very uncomfortable and embarrassed. In fact we went to Luby's, and Mary said that until they got paid, could I loan them enough money so they could eat.

She was a sweet lady; she was always a dear. A dear, sweet soul, and very talented, if you go back and listen to that stuff. Never intended to have a singing career. This woman did not have a mean bone in her body. Even messy and messed up and not having her stuff together, you could tell that this was just a dear, dear person. She didn't have an easy time of it. Nothing was easy for her.

I was very lucky to have known her, and very proud to

have been placed in the position of trust that she put me in, at a period of time where quite literally, it was her life. She really wanted to try to make it, and struggled and fought the good fight, but it just wasn't good enough.

She was very bitter, very hurt, very angry. This was something that she carried with her all the time. She was very disappointed and hurt with Berry, much more than he ever would have thought.

Toward the end, several Motown stars came to her aid financially.

Including Berry. For what he coulda, shoulda done, it was small. But at the time it was significant. It was a ceremonial gesture, certainly. It should have been more, and it should be to this day. Her kids should be getting every penny of royalties that that catalog is earning. They should not be paupers. They should not be destitute. Whatever there was should have been straightened out, and Berry should have been a *mensch*.

The best thing they could do is go back retroactively, and be gracious and return her rights to the royalties, to the income stream, to those children and her heirs. And just pay them. Ten percent royalty, something. They're making a fortune off her, to this minute, to this day. It's the unkindest cut.

It's not enough that [Gordy] called her the First Lady of Motown, that and a quarter is a quarter. How does that feed her kids? I have real pain about that because I know how hard her kids are struggling, and I know what Mary went through.

Mary sounded great. Until she got the throat cancer, Mary sounded damn good. She'd hit that stage, and you'd never know there was a wreck behind her. Mary always hit the stage like a lady and ready to perform. She was an excellent performer, she had all the poise and charisma, she knew how to show, and I never saw her do a bad show until she got sick, and that's because her throat was going. Try singing with throat cancer.

She cleaned up [from drugs] while she was in radiation therapy because somebody, namely me, offered her the ability to get the help. Which is all this woman ever needed, some-body to run interference. Because she had a lot of people in her camp who were using her, taking advantage of her and her income-earning ability. They know who they are. They know who took advantage of her and worked her like a dog. And took her to buy drugs, instead of taking her for treatment.

While going through radiation therapy, this woman went into a heroin detox program at St. Joseph's Hospital [in Burbank, California], and kicked, cleaned up; she was going to twelve-step meetings, and the whole bit. She wanted to live, she wanted the help. The hardest thing about getting Mary the help was getting [her away] from all the people who enjoyed taking advantage of her in her altered condition. They were male and female alike, and they know who they are.

She was very courageous, very dignified. She was very

poised. I can't even begin to explain what this woman went through, with the cancer. What she endured, with the tracheotomy. Not having any medical insurance, at least not being qualified, initially, for AFTRA [the American Federation of Television and Radio Artists, a union that also represents lead singers].

Being in a charity ward, being evicted from her place, having a four-year-old child, not having anything to fall back on. It was unbelievable, and she was such a dear. She was at one point hallucinating, and really going through a bad time. She was so sweet and funny, and so positive. She brought air into the room, as bad as it was—the chemotherapy, losing her hair.

But there were times, when Mary Wells looked better, sick, with the tracheotomy, than she had in years. She got her hair done, she lost a lot of weight, she looked fabulous. She became very conscientious about her clothing and makeup. [After] all the things she had given up when she was doing drugs, she would not go out if her makeup wasn't perfect and her hair wasn't together if her life depended on it. She came back to the old Mary.

She had a sense of pride and dignity about her, and she was really an inspiration. She fixed her relationship with her [older] children that had been strained. They rallied around her, they brought her a lot of peace of mind and contentment. Poor thing, she really wanted to live, and she didn't have a lot of help.

After the first radiation therapy, the first biopsy showed there was no cancer left. They thought she was clean, they thought they had gotten it. Unfortunately, somebody [whom Moore declined to identify] re-entered her life who insisted on smoking cigarettes around her in a closed car. That person also insisted on doing drugs and taking her into the neighborhood and to the drug dealers. This person, in my opinion, contributed considerably to her relapse.

This opinion was shared by her doctors, who were absolutely devastated when they found a spot on her lung. But this person had been warned not to do these things around her, or to her. Second-hand smoke, at a period of time when she was really and truly susceptible. When her body needed every break it could get, she didn't get it. She was lonely, she was scared, she had a weakness for this person, and she wound up realizing what a mistake she was making, but unfortunately at that point, she was terminal.

She'd quit smoking, she'd quit doing drugs, she was taking vitamins and doing everything humanly possible to live. But she made an error in judgment.

The Rhythm & Blues Foundation stepped in to help a destitute Wells with a well-publicized Mary Wells Fund. Seemingly every newspaper in the U.S. ran the story about musicians such as Bruce Springsteen, the Temptations, and Rod Stewart contributing to the fund.

There is no fund now for her kids. It was a nuisance to [The Rhythm & Blues Foundation], the Mary Wells Fund. Mary knew what I had done to try and save Jackie. And that endeared her to me, and me to her. Although we didn't know until later, when we got to talking girl talk, that we "shared" Jackie.

Moore first realized that Mary Wells was in dire trouble when the singer called her from the pay phone in the charity ward of Los Angeles County Hospital.

It was late July or early August, and she told me she had just had a tracheotomy. She called to tell me she was in trouble and needed help, and that Curtis would call me. So Curtis called, he explained that she had been diagnosed pre-cancerous, that they'd had to give her a tracheotomy, that she had pneumonia and no insurance, she needed help, was there anything I could do? Mary knew I was part of the Rhythm & Blues Foundation, because she had been one of the first grantees, at the Smithsonian Institution.

So she knew enough to put out an SOS. Also, Bruce Springsteen was in the studio, doing the *Human Touch* album. He wanted to use Mary on the album. But by that time, unbeknownst to him, she couldn't do it because something was wrong with her throat.

That's why Mary was never able to go into the studio with Bruce. Next, Bruce did something he hardly ever does. He made a public contribution to the Rhythm & Blues Foundation, to a fund that was declared to be the Mary Wells Fund. He went public with it, he actually did a media release, that there was this fund, and after that, there was an amazing outpouring of assistance to help Mary. Then I got on the phone and I got hold of Mary Wilson, and she got hold of Berry Gordy, and

they agreed to do something, and Rod Stewart contributed—
we made enough to cover some of her medical expenses.

In L.A., I met with the director of AFTRA's pension and
welfare fund, we went through Mary's stuff. He realized that
Mary should have been qualified [for health insurance]. They
got her straightened out and eventually ended up paying the
bulk of her treatment costs.

Then what happened was Mary had no place to live,
no way to take care of her children. And so it was really
a tremendous effort. What gave the Rhythm & Blues
Foundation credibility was their Mary Wells Fund. Finally,
they grudgingly agreed to give a little bit more money. Then
we ended up paying two months of Mary's rent ourselves,
out of our pockets. They owed me reimbursement money.
I was taking Mary to detox, to rehab, to chemotherapy. I
practically gave up my life for a time.

Mary was coming to our home in Arizona on the weekends because she wanted to be somewhere where she felt like
a human. She wanted to feel active and alive again. Arizona
was close enough, and [her doctor] had a corresponding
physician nearby, so we had somewhere to take her if she
needed immediate treatment. She was working on her book
with Steve Bergsman, who lives down here. She'd come down
here, and she'd sit outside and look at the stars at night.

To this day, if I go outside and the sky is filled with stars,
I call them "Mary's stars." Oh, yeah. She fell in love with the
night sky here; she was really happy and at peace. She was
really hopeful. She was even talking about going out and
doing track dates, lip-synching. She was the bravest person

I ever met. I hope that I never go through what I saw her go through. But I pray that if I do, I do it with as much class and grace as she did.

I went with her the first day that she had to have the radiation therapy on her throat. Can you imagine what it's like for a singer to know that they're getting ready to fry your vocal cords? I was in the room where the radiation machines were, at University of Arizona Cancer Center North. I went out of the room at the point they were ready to dose her. I went out of there knowing they were getting ready to nuke her. Her physician, Dr. Streeter, gave me a big old bear hug and tried to reassure me. And we tried to reassure each other that it was going to be OK to do this to her.

She was petrified, she was so scared, poor baby, but she took it. When her neck started turning black, we went and got makeup to cover it.

I miss her. She touched my heart, she touched my life. I hope that I'm a better person for it. I get sad every time I hear one of her songs on the radio. The one time I feel better, I feel uplifted, is when I look up and see Mary's stars. It makes me feel like she's still with us somehow.

Chapter Five
—*The Marvelettes*—

INKSTER IS ONE OF several Detroit suburbs with direct ties to the automotive industry. It was developed as a bedroom community for black Ford Motor Company workers; thus, an almost entirely black suburb came about, years before blacks were able to move in any numbers into the other suburbs of Detroit.

The history of the Marvelettes is deeply rooted in Inkster; to this day the group's members feel that they were slighted at Motown because of their small town, suburban origins.

But these suburban "hicks" had the last laugh. Their single "Please, Mr. Postman" not only was Motown's first No. 1 hit, and its second million-seller ("Shop Around" by the Miracles sold a million first), infusing much-needed cash into Berry Gordy's coffers, but they were part of the first wave of black girl groups that crossed over so completely they utterly seduced the white teenaged record-buying public.

If you were anywhere near a radio in 1961 and heard "Please, Mr. Postman," you were witnessing, perhaps for the first time, the pop-R&B, uptown-downtown, urban-suburban blend that became Motown's trademark, and was no less than revolutionary at the time. The Marvelettes, like many Motown groups of the time, erased racial lines and created a new sort of omniracial teenaged voice, an iconic teen with a feverish interest in the opposite sex, dating, dances, and all the sexually repressed, innocent pastimes of the early sixties.

The group had not one but two strong lead singers. Gladys Horton was the sassy lead voice of "Please, Mr. Postman," "Beechwood 4-5789," and other teenaged hits, while the voice of Wanda Young (who later married Bobby Rogers of the Miracles) had a haunting, smoky quality that was perfect for later, more subtle songs such as "Don't Mess With Bill," "The Hunter Gets Captured By The Game," and "My Baby Must Be A Magician." It was Young's baby-sexy voice that intrigued Smokey Robinson so much that he composed the last three songs specifically for her.

The original quintet of Marvelettes, as signed by Motown, was Gladys Horton, Katherine Anderson (later, Schaffner), Wanda Young (later, Rogers), Juanita Cowart and Georgianna Tillman. Cowart was the first to leave, in 1962, and Tillman departed in 1965 when she married Billy Gordon of the Contours, leaving the group a trio.

When Motown moved west in 1970, it essentially abandoned several groups in Detroit, including the Marvelettes, the original and quintessential girl group. Marriage effectively rendered the group defunct for enough years that they lost the rights to their name to a sharp operator who in the nineties had several groups of non-original

"Marvelettes" touring. Meanwhile, original singer Gladys Horton struggled to field her own group and support her disabled son.

A brief reunion in 1990 with Horton, Schaffner, and Rogers came to naught. In the ensuing years, Schaffner retired from show business, and Rogers has been too ill to perform or grant interviews. Horton was wary of press intrusion, refusing to comment much to journalists over the years. She did tell me her side of the "fake Marvelettes" story, in 1998. "You want to hear a sad story?" she quipped. "I'll give you sad . . . I have a handicapped son. Every time he puts a group out there, he's taking money out of my pocket." Horton died in January 2011, aged 66.

—Katherine Anderson Schaffner—

Inkster is west of Detroit; we're located between Detroit and Ann Arbor. It's a small community. We all lived in the same area, except for Gladys—Juanita, Georgianna, Wanda, and myself.

We all sang in the [Inkster High] school glee club; that was one of the classes we had together. They announced that they were having a talent show. When they announced that, Gladys asked why don't we go ahead and be a part of the talent show. At that point we began rehearsing our little songs and things of that nature. We sang one of the Chantels' numbers—I'm thinking it was "Maybe." That's a song that sticks out.

We lost! But because of our performance, one of our teachers, a Mrs. Shirley Sharpley, when it came time to audition for Motown, because that was a part of what your winnings would be, to audition for Motown, she recommended that they take the top five. And we were fourth.

Berry Gordy had just started Motown, but already several writer-producer teams were forming.

Brian [Holland] and those were writing, but not to the magnitude that Robert Bateman was, as a writer, and Mickey Stevenson. They were the ones who worked up "Please, Mr. Postman." Robert and Brian usually combined their names into "Brianbert" to work together.

We were still in high school when "Please, Mr. Postman," our first record, was out. It was written by a William Garrett, who lived here in Inkster. One of the girls who was part of the talent show with us, her name was Georgia Dobbins, well Wanda [Young] Rogers replaced Georgia, because Georgia did not wish to sing. I think she was thinking in terms of getting married. So Wanda was chosen to come into the group and take her place.

We knew William Garrett because Inkster being a small area, that was one of the things he had done. Well, anyway, like most of his songs, "Please, Mr. Postman" was in a bluesy manner, so Georgia Dobbins helped to reconstruct the song lyrically as well as musically.

You had to come with an original [song] to Motown, so we brought "Please, Mr. Postman." They never thought suburbanites could do it.

The Marvelettes in 1966, as a trio. Left to right:
Katherine Anderson Schaffner, Wanda Rogers, and Gladys Horton.

Unlike many of the Detroit artists, once we hit, we hit, with our songs. Many of the artists who were there from Detroit, they had a bit of a problem with it. I don't know if Berry had a problem with it, but it somewhat seemed that way. Because we were girls from the suburbs, not from the city, and we came in there with the song that was their first million-seller. I don't recall that we had as much participation in our career, as I look back at it, through the years, as did many of the Detroit artists. That's the mentality of big city vs. suburbia.

I don't think we were supported and necessarily promoted in the same manner that many of the other artists were. But because of our own repertoire of music, and us as individuals, that was the reason that we were able to do some of the things that we did. We had a great support factor. Our support factor came from the fans of the world. So with it being from the fans of the world, at that point in time they couldn't hold us back, because our popularity was great with the fans.

The Marvelettes racked up the hits. Beyond "Please, Mr. Postman," there's a deep well of singles that were snapped up by the fabled Young America: "Too Many Fish In The Sea," "As Long As I Know He's Mine," "Playboy," and more. Most of these achievements were posted when Diana Ross was still flouncing around West Grand Boulevard, practicing her pout.

It was before anybody else did anything. They were there, the Supremes and all. They just couldn't understand how we, from a hick town like Inkster, could come in and get a hit before they did. It was like a big city-suburban mentality. As I look around now, you still see that kind of thing.

The Marvelettes were very young.

When we recorded "Please, Mr. Postman" we were

[mostly] 16; Gladys was 15. Wanda had already graduated from high school.

In comparison with groups such as the Chantels and the Shirelles, the difference with the Marvelettes was that we were more upbeat. The sister groups like the Chantels and the Shirelles did more slow, ballad-type music. We did more fast-paced, upbeat music.

The Marvelettes were soon sent out on the road, both with the early, more rustic versions of the Motown Revues, and with Dick Clark's Caravan of Stars bus tours.

I loved going on the road. As with many artists who lived in the black community at that time, it was an avenue that allowed you to travel to other cities and states, and gave you that "out." In doing so it also helped you to grow. Oftentimes, when you stay in your own community, you think differently. If you stay within the confines of your familiar surroundings, then you have a tendency to think as the surroundings dictate.

That being the case, you never step out further because you don't know anything different than the confines of your own surroundings. Show business allowed us to travel to any number of states, which meant we were able to make friends in those areas. It broadened our horizons.

Show business allowed you to meet people from all walks of life. In the long term, I've always been able to communicate with people, but it allowed me a broader span. I can deal with anybody on any level.

In comparison with young people today, many of them

don't get out of their own area, so they don't necessarily know how to deal with people from all walks of life.

It's part of the Motown myth that everybody went through the famous Motown charm school. But early artists like the Marvelettes, the Miracles, and Mary Wells didn't have the luxury of wardrobe mistresses and choreographers when they got hit records.

In the later years, we got training from Motown. In the early years, our choreography and all that were done by the individual artists. Not until maybe '65, '66 did we really begin to get more into the artist development department. But by then we'd already been out there for several years. So much of your choreography and such were done by the artists themselves. In later years, that's when you had the Cholly Atkins choreography. He polished up what you did and added more finesse to what you were doing, as well as, of course, bringing in more ideas from his era.

The camaraderie between the early Motown acts was intense.

We were close to Bobby Rogers of the Miracles [who eventually married Wanda] and of course Claudette [Rogers Robinson] because when we were out there on the road, Claudette and Mary Wells were the only women who were out there with us on the Motown tours. And, of course, Martha and the Vandellas came along later.

We are known for more songs than "Please, Mr. Postman." Not in the industry per se, because most of the time, when we're publicized about a CD set or a cassette set, or something, usually the only song they use off that is "Please, Mr. Postman." However, the Marvelettes have had any number of songs that were in the Top 10, or the Top 20.

"Too Many Fish In The Sea," "Danger" . . . You always have to have "Please, Mr. Postman" because that's the one that allowed Motown to move into the area they wanted, because it was their first crossover record. So our popularity, when we first started, crossed over. We weren't just for black audiences, but both white and black. "Please, Mr. Postman" was the one that spread across the board to both. That was the one that broke down the color barrier.

Wanda sings lead on the later songs. Gladys sang much of our earlier stuff because she had the voice, more or less, that they were looking for. Gladys had more of a commercial sound; that also helped as far as the Marvelettes were concerned. We were unique in that we did have two lead singers. But originally, in the talent show, I was the one who sang lead. With five voices, you could get five different keys in there, to tighten up your sound.

The Marvelettes really had several careers; the early girl group songs including the high energy Norman Whitfield-produced "Too Many Fish In The Sea," then the later, more mature Smokey Robinson-penned hits including "Don't Mess With Bill," "My Baby Must Be A Magician," and "The Hunter Gets Captured By The Game." It all came to an end with the close of the sixties.

The group—I don't know if we necessarily disbanded. What happened is we weren't recording. It ended up being a lot of internal problems, in 1970. Motown was in the process of moving west, as well.

That was their decision to move west, and you shouldn't have to make a decision based upon the company making that kind of decision, because there are too many things involved outside of your career itself. Your family, your friends, everything you know is in the area.

Katherine Schaffner is one of the few Motown singers who prefers retirement, and insists she didn't want to reform her old group, even in the eighties, when Gladys tried to launch a reunion.

No, I didn't want to. When you go into something at that age, one of the things that I was able to do and some people have not been able to do is resolve myself that this was a very important part of my life at that point in time, but in order for me to progress, I have to move on in more ways than one. That also means careerwise. Because when you see the handwriting on the wall, then you need to attend to what's going on around you. I had gone into meditation and prayer sessions with myself, so that when it did conclude, I was perfectly fine with it.

I didn't do anything but raise my children. Yes, I went to a bigger job! Primarily, I was a stay-at-home wife. And I raised my older children.

There are, of course, the non-original Marvelettes touring all over the place. They've even shared a bill with the Temptations. Gladys Horton, the original lead singer, the voice behind "Please, Mr. Postman," couldn't legally use the name "Marvelettes" because the name was trademarked.

There are several groups touring as the Marvelettes.

We're in the process of picking up new fans; they're people who were not even born, not even a glimmer in their parents' eye, when we recorded. These new generations of fans are not familiar with who the artists really are. That being the case, it allows for the bogus groups to be able to succeed; because fans are just interested in seeing their favorite artists, that's what allows for these different groups to be able to thrive.

I have very strong feelings about it. They can go around saying that they're original and all that. First of all, they're not original, none of them ever have been, or ever will be, and of course with the different artists' bios and the information they have, they're able to get that information from their bios, and they're able to go on and do shows because of the public being naive.

The general public is very naive; they don't know who the real artists are. There's no way necessarily that you can stop it. The other problem that I have, I think it's asinine that promoters book the bogus acts. Some of them don't know that they're not the originals because the promoters and disc jockeys aren't of that era.

So it makes it hard for Gladys, who's been trying to travel and perform, do it, when she's an original Marvelette! I don't think it should be to the point where she has to fight to use the name that she made possible. And popular.

I don't feel that original artists should have to go through any changes with anybody in order to perform. But it's the naiveté of those who book the shows. But they also make no effort to check to see if it's the original act or not.

None of them have ever been, or ever will be. There's only one Marvelettes.

Marvin Gaye had an early Marvelettes connection; he wrote "Beechwood 4-5789" and plays drums on "Please, Mr. Postman."

Marvin was a very talented artist. There was so much talent at Motown. You know, Steve Holsey of the *Michigan Chronicle* [the African-American owned Detroit paper] ran a survey, and different people were saying, just here in the city, Motown could have continually thrived as a record company—it's more or less on a decline now—because of its stable of artists from the sixties. That's what's keeping them alive in the nineties.

The catalog from old Motown is what's making Motown thrive. Because people are continually buying the re-released stuff. Hindsight is always a hundred percent, but I thought this then: Why not keep the studios and things like that here, because there's any number of people here in this area, not just Detroit but the east coast, northeast, and central; that's all untapped talent. When you move the whole shebang out to California, then you eliminate all the artists that are here.

To take it and shut down everything, for a hope and a dream of going into another area, that's fine. But that's putting the cart before the horse. If you've got the horse, you move to California. Things didn't necessarily develop into anything, the music aspect of it. There weren't that many [Motown] artists to come out of California.

Most of the house band, the Funk Brothers, didn't go to California—except for James Jamerson.

None of them hardly, although there were a few that did go to California. But the bulk mass of them stayed here in the Detroit area. Having worked together any number of years, then, of course, they knew each other, they knew how each other played. They still play together in jazz bands, some of them, here in the area. Therefore, you shot the horse! Motown became Motown because of its musicians and artists. Motown became Motown because of Berry's dream, but a dream doesn't get you very far if you don't have the talent. The talent is what helped make Motown what it was.

If he wanted to go into films, that would have been fine. Go into films, and have that division. But don't close up total shop here.

A lot of the artists did move to California, but it didn't

make for better success for them there. Their success was here. That's why I was very happy to read that [then-Motown CEO] Andre Harrell wanted to bring Motown back to Detroit [Harrell was fired from Motown in 1997]. There are so many talented young people here who will never get the opportunity to go to New York or California. So why not be where your masses of people are? Why not be where your untapped talent is?

The other side of it is, when things are meant to happen, they're meant to happen in a specific location. And so therefore, it was meant for Detroit to become Motown. Maybe the reason that things began to falter for them was because you're taking something that was meant to be and changing it. And when you're changing it, you broke your luck.

It's almost as if Motown forgot the music that put it on the map.

Motown has never recognized or has given the Marvelettes their just due, for the contribution that we made to the foundation and building of Motown. They have never, ever—and we're damn near going into the year 2000. They've never given us credit, these little hick girls from Inkster, and we are the ones who officially have the first No. 1. It's always been said that the Miracles did [with "Shop Around"]. But the Miracles didn't until ours began to hit, and it's been documented in any number of publications.

We were not even invited to the *Motown 25* show [which aired on NBC in 1983]. Any number of different artists were, and I don't know if it's because we're an inactive group. But even if we weren't going to perform, we at least should have been invited. That's the difference between people who are in Los Angeles, and people who are here. People in L.A. don't have a clue who the early Motown artists were if they were not associated with them in L.A. The invitation wasn't even extended for us to be invited guests. When you eliminate some of your history, you have a problem later on.

Chapter Six
—Martha Reeves—

IN THE MIDDLE OF a Detroit winter, Martha Reeves, cosseted in fox fur, enters her favorite restaurant, Fishbone's, in downtown Detroit. She may not be politically correct, but she is the quintessential Motown diva.

"A diva must have her furs," Reeves teases as she sinks into a chair, pulling the fur up around her neck. "I catch cold easily, and running from a warm club into the cold air, that'll get you sick."

Some time later, when I caught up with her again at Fishbone's, it was spring, and Reeves brought her pride and joy, her twenty-six-year-old son Eric.

In a world where glamour and Motown divas are in especially short supply, it's somehow comforting that Reeves is still in Detroit, still ready at the drop of a wig to lend the sort of star presence only a female schooled in the Motown style of presentation can give to fundraisers and charity events. Sequins, attitude, the flashy smile, dramatic makeup, but nothing that takes away from the essential, dishy girlishness. It's the sort of attitude that leads Reeves to tease a waiter who knew one of her past boyfriends, "Do you believe he said that to me?"

It's ironic that she is one of Motown's enduring icons, because when the company was in full swing, she was caught in a classic case of sibling rivalry. Reeves was the talented but overlooked daughter, while Diana Ross was the favored child given all the breaks.

Reeves persisted, virtually willing herself into stardom, caught as she was in a situation where there were countless talented females—too many.

She hit with a more soulful sound than the Supremes, and that is probably her greatest legacy. Female singers gush about the Supremes' lush life image, but it's those wild Vandellas hits that everybody wanted to sing. "Dancing In The Street," "Nowhere To Run," "Jimmy Mack," "Heatwave," "Quicksand"—Motown may have been the pop crossover company, but Martha's wail was loud and earthy.

Like most Motowners, Reeves is a Detroiter with deep roots in the South. She was born to Ruby and Elijah Reeves in Eufaula, Alabama, in 1941, but moved with them to the Motor City when she was a baby. She graduated from Northeastern High School. It was Ruby Reeves who inspired Martha to try harder than everybody else.

As the oldest of twelve children, Reeves wasn't used to being coddled. Her hard-working father supported the family with jobs at Packard, Ford, and then the city of Detroit's water department. He was incensed when he found out she was working at Motown for free. Elijah Reeves bought his daughter a '57 Chevy when she finally stood up to her boss,

Mickey Stevenson, and asked for a salary—thirty-five
dollars a week—in 1962.

She had been working at a dry cleaners by day and
doing five-dollar gigs at places like the 20 Grand by night.
It was at the 20 Grand that Stevenson caught her act. But
he claimed he couldn't record her just yet. So she went to
Motown and made herself useful. It wasn't yet time for
Martha and the Vandellas.

—*Mickey Stevenson*—

Martha was a wonderful person. She wanted me to
record her at Motown. At the time we had, in my opinion, too
many girl groups, so I wasn't interested in recording her. But I
liked her as a person. She said, "Look, I just want to be around
and work with you over there." So she ended up being my
secretary. And she was very good at that, I might add. Because
she was the type of person, if I stayed 'til one in the morning,
she stayed 'til one in the morning.

So we got this song for Kim Weston called "Dancing In
The Street," I remember. And Martha did the demo for us. And
forget it, that did it! It was absolutely perfect! It was a great
marriage between her and that song. She'd done a few things
before that, but we still weren't leaning on pushing Martha,
because we had so many other artists. It wasn't Martha's fault,
it was just at the time, limited airplay on the radio with black
records, you could only get so many on, all over the country,
and you could only get so many *girls* on. We came out with

too many girls, they would not get played, no matter what we did. So we had to kind of space these things, and she was just not in that group.

But her persistence, and her willingness to stick it out, was incredible. It made me kind of feel guilty. So when something came along, it was a marriage, and it worked. At the time I think, I was even going with Kim. But it was just Martha's time.

Surely Kim Weston wanted "Dancing In The Street" for herself.

No. She had no problem. She had me, she didn't have a problem! Martha wore that song out, too. That was something about us at Motown that was really great. No matter whether it was my song, or your song, or a Four Tops tune, or the Tempts did it; when we heard a song and it was clickin', that was it! We backed off. That one belonged to that person, and we'd all agree to that. And that was the end of it. I think that was one of the gifts that the Lord gave to that organization.

In Reeves' book Dancing In The Street, she held back from any major league dissing of any of her Motown colleagues, even Berry Gordy. She isn't sorry, she says.

—Martha Reeves—

I love the book. I'm glad I've refrained from being angry, and I didn't gossip, and I didn't put anything in my book that would hurt anybody. I'm glad I did that. It didn't sell like it should have sold because I didn't put anything dirty or rotten in there, but then, I wasn't trying to sell books, I was trying to clean myself of all the information I had, to set the record straight.

A lot of people have written books with a lot of lies in it. So if they want to believe anybody, maybe they'll come to the source.

We used to sit down and talk: Mary Wells, David Ruffin, Eddie Kendricks, Marvin Gaye, Tammi Terrell, Florence Ballard. We always said that we'd write this down, because nobody would believe the things that we went through, as kids, on that bus, trying to become famous. And they didn't get a chance.

So I said before something happens that I can't control, I'd better get this book out of me. Now I got the second book, and I think I know how to write it. Oh yes. I started it and it'll take maybe a year. Last time I rushed, I gathered things in a hurry. This time I'll take my time, work on my own with a word processor, and get it to the point where once it's edited, the truth will stay in.

Reeves does admit that her relationship with Berry

Gordy could be rocky. She resented the way he favored the Supremes.

[Gordy] and I have sat and talked about this. He admitted to me that our relationship wasn't the best, that he favored the Supremes because they would do what he said. See, I would always be the one who asked questions.

I've always admired him. He was a mystery man. You know he'd do something, but you didn't know what. I believed in him and I trusted in him. Everybody wanted to please Berry.

I can't find many bad things to say about Motown. Very little.

And yet Reeves had to sue them for unpaid royalties a few years back.

We were allowed a certain percentage of our earnings. It was only after the company left Detroit for Los Angeles in 1972 that I stopped getting paid. In 1989, I started getting royalties again.

I wrote to Berry Gordy in a letter the other day, "You treated your women well." Had it not been for him, I would not have been discovered. I don't care what people say, he's a fair man. And he's got a good heart.

I've never seen him drunk, I've never seen him smoke a cigarette, and to be honest, I've never heard him use profanity. I've seen him angry, but I've never heard him really just curse. And that means a lot to me, because having dealt with people all over the world, I know how you can be once you're at the point where you're spending millions and you've acquired millions of dollars. You don't owe anybody anything. But this man still has a heart, after all the time, and all the money that he's created and all the millionaires he's created. He's still a decent man.

Gordy was surrounded by so many strong women in his own family, perhaps he didn't know any other way to treat women than as equals.

Yes, yes, yes. And the women that he chose were the women who came to him, basically. And some of them were good for him, and some of them were not good for him. But he was good for the artists, and that's the only way I know him, as an artist and manager and record company owner. We've become real good friends over the years, and if I want to, I can call him and I can talk to him about anything. And I like that. A lot of people are afraid to talk to him, they think that he owes them things. If they do, they should confront him because I'm sure he'll give them satisfaction.

It's time for the bad report to die, and his good to shine, because he did a lot of good. And Detroit reflects it. Because every time I look around, there's a Motown record shop or a Motown cafe or a Motown supermarket or car wash . . . that he's represented. And he made up that word, Motown. So I'm especially proud of him.

Reeves credits Gordy for the artist development grooming she received. Cholly Atkins taught choreography,

Maurice King and others would work on vocals, and Maxine Powell would fine-tune their grooming, deportment, and stage presence.

When I wrote to [Gordy], I said, "I am so glad that you took good care of your women." He got [modeling and etiquette teacher] Mrs. [Maxine] Powell for us, and everything. I was in the play, *Ain't Misbehavin'*, and I looked at the pictures, and I looked at how I presented myself, [compared to] the girls who didn't have Mrs. Powell, it shows. They don't know how to stand, they don't know how to walk, they don't know how to present themselves, they're not lady-like.

Martha and the Vandellas: Left to right, Rosalind Ashford-Holmes, Annette Beard, and Martha.

Berry knew. He saw what we needed and got it for us. He didn't just sit back and say [*gruff* voice] "Oh, those girls are OK, but they're a bit raunchy, or they're a little wild." He remedied the problem. And he taught us, like the steps that Cholly Atkins taught; that was all theater.

When Mrs. Powell and I got together last Saturday, she gave me some new steps! On the dance floor. I said, "Mrs. Powell, why didn't you give me these when I first started working with you?" She said, "You weren't ready for it."

She had to teach us how to walk, how to dance. She's still the loveliest person that I've ever known. We didn't take her seriously when we first met her, but I'll always be indebted to her. I had to grow up, too.

Berry knew how to build an artist. Once he got to a point, it was up to you to take the lessons and go on and do your job, and keep yourself on your own feet, or you'd fall by the wayside if you didn't continue. [Then] what you learned was a waste of time. I learned how it works, what you need to succeed. And they gave us everything we needed. Everything. We didn't have common sense, but he couldn't help us with that. But everything else, if they thought we needed it, we got it.

Especially Mrs. [Esther Gordy] Edwards, [sister of Berry; a Motown executive, and in the early days, a tour chaperone] she deserves a lot of credit because she paid more attention to us than anyone else. Berry would give her instructions and she would carry it out. She would go on the road with us, she would chaperone us, she hung out. She rode the bus with us, she didn't fly and meet us there, she was right there with us.

It's hilarious that on those Motown Revues, it fell to a musician, Thomas "Beans" Bowles, who was bandleader and played flute and saxophone with the Motown band, to go around to all the hotel rooms making sure the Motown stars were in their beds at night.

We had a 94-one-nighter tour, and along about the thirtieth night, we were all getting a little too familiar with each other. I can say that I wasn't guilty! I shared a room with Mary Wells, and I remember it vividly: The door was opened, the flashlight shone into the room, and there I was in bed, probably with drool coming out of my mouth and rollers in my hair.

But some of my stablemates were caught in the act of partying—playing music, disturbing their next-door neighbors, sitting around in their pajamas. We were all adults, of course, but they wanted us to get our rest.

Some of the most memorable Motown Revue shows were in Detroit, at the Fox Theatre on Woodward Avenue. On the night of July 23, 1967, when the deadly Detroit riots broke out, Reeves happened to be performing at the Fox.

We were at the Fox Theatre and "Jimmy Mack" had just been released, and I was anxious to sing it because I thought it was the best song I'd ever done. But they told us that we had to stop the show and tell everybody to go home, that there was a police curfew. And there were sirens, and guns going off. We managed to get home. Then I had to get on an airplane, while the city burned, to go to South Carolina.

One Detroit radio station played Martha and the Vandellas records during that hot July week with the idea that it would calm listeners down. Perhaps it was more of a distraction than a calming influence. Mary Wells' records would have been calming.

It was a beautiful feeling, when we were full of hate and anger and everybody was so full of unrest, that we saw people actually join together, get out of their cars and dance to a song ["Dancing In The Street"] that meant we should rejoice. I can recall it quite vividly, seeing people open up their college campuses and let us dance on their football fields. The Motown sound was a very big influence in the civil rights movement. It was not that we marched or paraded; we just promoted it through love. It's easy making love.

And yet "Dancing In The Street" was banned in some other riot-torn cities that summer, for it was feared that Reeves was "calling out around the world" for people to riot.

That hurt my feelings so very badly. What I related the song to was my experiences in Rio at Carnival time, and in New Orleans at Mardi Gras. It was a time for people to forget who they are and just get with each other to be happy and loving and dance and rejoice. It was a celebration, related to spiritual things. My musical partners at Motown and I, we helped in letting people know that it was all right to feel anger, but you have to go from there and find an answer, and it's love. We're dreamers, yes, but there's a peace in that dream. That everybody can get along.

After her string of sixties hits, as the decade wound down, Reeves saw Vandellas come and go. As Motown's attention turned increasingly to the Supremes, the best producers and the best songs were steered to that group. Reeves' increasing isolation culminated in her being left behind, like many others, when Motown moved to Los Angeles in the early seventies. Martha moved to Los Angeles on her own and struggled for a while as a solo artist, but she returned to Detroit in the early eighties.

She still frets about the persistent rumor that she suffered a nervous breakdown in the seventies. She freely admits to having had a drug problem, mostly prescription, she says, and [that's] a thing of the past.

I did not have a nervous breakdown. I wasn't born with a nervous problem. Most of it was prescribed drugs—and my dad hipped me to the danger in that when he saw all the bottles I had. It was similar to what happened to Elvis Presley. When he wanted to wake up, he'd take something. When he wanted to go to sleep, something else. And you're getting stuff from different doctors in different towns.

I've always made myself available to the press. And you know, they could have destroyed me. They all knew about my drug problem, but they didn't write about it. I think they knew I'd beat it and come through.

Drugs have always been around the music business, and especially in the late sixties and early seventies at Motown, as in the rest of the entertainment world, they were considered an accepted outlet or recreation.

There was pressure on us because you get thrown into a crowd of people, and you don't know who's a friend or who's a foe. You don't know. You're singing about love, you're out there on your own, you meet a lot of attractive and very sensual men. And you want to belong, so you hang with them, and what they do usually rubs off on you.

There was no pressure personally, but you did want to be with the "in crowd." You did want to do what the big guys do. And being new artists, we didn't know. That was my fault, being curious. I can't blame it on anybody. But I do know that it's something I had to go through, so I can look at people when they approach me with anything that isn't natural, and say, "No!"

But you're subservient to a degree because you whine and you sing and you coo and you purr and you pose. So silly things can come into your ear when you're in that state of mind.

My advice to young up-and-comings is to hang out with other professionals. Other professionals will tell you, they'll try to warn you of the downfalls of street drugs and outside influences. Most of the people who approached me with drugs were people who were trying to destroy Berry Gordy's empire. And our lives could have been lived as chess pieces. There were gambles made; in fact, there are some girls running around calling themselves the Marvelettes, and they say they won their name in a gambling game. That's why this horse-shaker [the person who trademarked the name "Marvelettes," taking it away from the real group], whatever his name is, can solicit work for them.

And Otis Williams [of the Temptations] is hiring these fake girls, because they're the only Marvelettes working! The other Marvelettes don't work regularly. And some of them will never overcome their drug effects.

A recurring theme in the life story of so many female singers seems to be the "falling for a bad man" scenario.

The heart is a funny thing. You can't predict who you're going to fall in love with, or how you're going to be affected by some people. I remember trying to get pregnant by a guy I just admired so much for his talent. He didn't like me. But I admired his talent, so I wanted to have a baby by him. So I pulled at him and tugged at him, and he always said to me, "I have nothing to offer you." But I wouldn't listen to him. Because I thought, if I was good enough to him, and if the songs that I sang made me fall in love with him, then one day he might have a change of heart or change of mind. No such thing! And you only learn that by living, and by getting older and realizing that if you don't love yourself, nobody else will love you.

So there's lessons that you have to learn, and nobody's in your ear telling you good things; people are always in your ear either trying to get with you, get your money, or destroy what you're doing. Because a lot of people can't do what you do, and don't like you doing it. For as many fans who come to you and want your autograph, there's that many who will stab you in the back and try to hurt you if you don't watch yourself.

As the official hometown Motown diva, Reeves is on call for everything. In the spring of 1997, she added diva presence to a wedding on the lawn at the Motown museum in Detroit.

I was on that lawn wedding detail. Did you hear about it? Some people came from Leeds, England, and wanted to be married at the Motown Museum. And I'm responsible for that. I met the girl seven years ago when she had broken up with an abusive husband. And she came to our soundcheck and sort of pushed her way in, and said, "I'm not leaving until I can speak to Martha Reeves." She had some Motown records that they had fallen in love with. She said, "This is all I have left of a bad marriage. If you just sign these for me, I'll probably never marry again. Life is too hard."

I said, "No, no no no, don't feel like that." Because there is love for everybody. Mama said, there's a mate for everything. Birds got mates. Animals have mates, and they don't have good sense. So like she said, hold out for the right one. And I shared that information with her. To show how just a little help when you're down counts, she came here to get married. And the guy is lovely, and he's well-to-do! So she not only has a good parent for her two girls, but she found her a good man.

And he's also a Motown fan—between them they have three thousand Motown records—and they brought a few over for me to sign! She was hoping that I would be in town. She took a chance. I got home two days before her wedding.

In the summer of 1997, having just come off a grueling tour with **Ain't Misbehavin'**, *Reeves was planning to make a record.*

I am going to do a gospel album. I lost my mom, and now I'm an orphan. I lost my daddy in '83; I lost my mom in '96. There's some songs that I think will heal me a little, of my losses, so yes, I am. And I'm working with several producers in town. I've been making inquiries now; in fact, all week long I've been trying to get into somebody's studio here in the city.

I want a record of my own. I want to produce it, I want the royalties, I want the publishing. I want the creative freedom because I've never had it. And I feel I'm old enough now to have my freedom.

Martha Reeves (in forefront) in the 1990s, with Vandellas
Rosalind Ashford-Holmes (left) and Lois Reeves.

"Motherless Child" is the first one I'll do. I think it's something that would heal me. Mama's favorite song was "What A Friend We Have In Jesus." And "Precious Lord." So those are three that I know I'll start with. Whenever I feel that there's a problem, I just hum one of those songs, and I feel things will work out.

That's why you learn those songs when you're small, 'cause they take you through your adulthood. Because you can't do anything without faith.

Reeves pulls out a cache of old pictures she's brought

along. One shows her in the sixties, with the Vandellas and the Beach Boys.

This picture is when the Beach Boys let us work with them. Is that Marvin Gaye back there? It was our first engagement in Detroit, after the Motown Revue. The record was just hitting, "Come And Get These Memories." We were featured as "Marvin Gaye and the Vandellas." We did one number, "Come And Get These Memories," then we stood onstage and waited 'til Marvin came, and he did "Hitchhike" and "Stubborn Kind Of Fellow." At the [Michigan] State Fair, with the Beach Boys. [*She points to the picture.*] One of these babies is real sick, and one is no longer with them. This is Mike Love. I've had a crush on him ever since. But they were kind enough. They had big records at the time, but they let us open their show.

Using her own experience in the school of hard knocks, Reeves says she'd like to work with young musicians to help steer them away from the sort of mistakes she made in her pop career.

I want to get involved with new talent. But there will never be another Berry Gordy or Motown, where you take a bunch of people, and everybody's wonderful, and everybody's working hard, for excellence. That will never happen again. And I'm glad to have been a part of that. I know what the feeling's like, and if I can ever instill that in anybody coming up, I will. But it's hard to share that with people who don't feel the way we felt in the early days. We sang, not for money, we sang to satisfy. [*She laughs*]. Now that we're old, we wish we'd sang more for money!

Reeves pulls out pictures of her mother Ruby's funeral, from the winter of 1996.

Mrs. Edwards gave me these pictures she took at my mother's funeral. Stevie Wonder sang at my mom's services. I heard the Lord's Prayer a million times, but never the way he sang it. He used to come over to my house after sessions at Motown. When they didn't pick him up, I'd take him home.

So he knew and loved my family just like he's a member. Because we took him in. It's not like he was a little blind kid. Stevie was active! Stevie would beat everybody up; he was taller than most of them. They'd tear my mama's house up. They made Stevie ride a bike. That's something he'll never forget.

Mrs. Edwards took these pictures. I couldn't see anybody for my grief. I didn't know who was there, so with these pictures she gave me insight into what was happening. Wonderful pictures. So people wonder, are we family at Motown? Yes, we are.

Here's [U.S. Rep.] John Conyers. Look at all the lovely flowers. Weddings are beautiful, funerals are not, but this was a beautiful funeral. And [the casket] was a lovely Rolls Royce that we got her. And these are the names of all of her twelve children, with doves.

Reeves is smoking her own rolled cigarettes, which can

*cause raised eyebrows from those who don't know what a
real marijuana joint looks like. Hers are pure tobacco.*

I'm smoking tobacco. No nicotine, and it's always moist
because I keep it in my own humidor. So I'm not really
damaging my lungs. Since we've been sitting here talking, you
haven't heard me rattling, there's no phlegm in my throat, I'm
in good shape. If it happens, then I'll put the cigarettes down.
I've been on echinachea and elderberry. Anything natural, I'm
on a natural kick. I've been buying the ginseng drinks.

*She peers outside Fishbone's into the neighborhood,
which borders Detroit's bustling Greektown sector.*

It sure is lovely to see this area, which used to be Black
Bottom [*Detroit's famed black entertainment district, razed to
make way for the freeway*], turn into a downtown area that's
worthy of the name downtown. I'm going to try to stay
in this area. I'm looking for a home. That building I'm in,
that's a co-op, and I'm ready to move to a home now, spread
things out and see what I have, and give them to the various
museums. The Rock and Roll Hall of Fame will give me a
whole showcase if I give them enough material! 'Cause I was
there for the opening and I have been a faithful participant
in their seminars.

*Reeves tried to live in Los Angeles for more than a
decade, moving out by herself after Motown left her behind.
But she ended up back in Detroit.*

When I was living in Los Angeles for those twelve years, when my son was young, I had to struggle to keep going because Motown did leave me here. Out there I was just another unemployed performer looking for a gig when I wasn't working. That's not true in Detroit. Here everybody knows me.

As if to demonstrate her point, a woman who'd just had "Happy Birthday" sung to her by Fishbone's waiters stopped by our table on her way out. "Why didn't you sing for my birthday?" she teases Reeves. "You didn't ask me!" Martha shrieks.

Chapter Seven
—The Supremes—

THE SUPREMES MAY HAVE slouched into the Motown offices on West Grand Boulevard in 1960 as four scrappy teenagers from the projects (they became a trio later), but just a few years in the Gordy dream factory turned them into urban goddesses, the culmination of the Motown dream, the huge crossover female act Berry Gordy dreamed about for years.

If, while wearing tight sheaths and glossy wigs, they were still willing and able to rumble with the other female groups backstage, well, that girlish grit was part of their Detroit-bred charm.

Gordy finally realized his dream in Diana Ross, Mary Wilson, and Florence Ballard, who were talented yet guileless enough to do whatever he and his top-notch creative staff demanded. Ross showed signs of diva temperament early on—her producers, the Holland brothers, Brian and Eddie, and Lamont Dozier knew to record her vocals on the first or second take, or she'd get cranky. She also worked tirelessly on herself, creating a larger than life persona that endures today and is so fabulous it doesn't need hit records or movies to endure.

In the mid-sixties, the Supremes were the epitome of pop genius. Here were three smiling girls dressed in shimmering bugle beads, coiffed within an inch of their lives, exuding a coltish feminine charm that survived the journey from the stage of the Ed Sullivan Theater into every sixties child's living room via television.

Their arms fluttering and hips swaying in choreographer Cholly Atkins' vision of spunky yet deferential femininity, the three cooed and sparkled their way through a catalog of seductively catchy Holland-Dozier-Holland songs: "Stop In The Name Of Love," "Baby Love," "My World Is Empty (Without You)," "You Can't Hurry Love," and "You Keep Me Hanging On," to name a few.

The hits didn't start right away, and the gowns were modest at first; Hudson's bargain basement and hand-sewn, rather than Hudson's Oval Room or Saks. Lynda Laurence, who became a Supreme in 1972, remembers seeing the Supremes early on, in her hometown of Philadelphia.

—Lynda Laurence—

I think it was impossible not to be a fan of the Supremes then. One of the first songs I remember hearing wasn't a major hit, but it got them to Philadelphia: "Buttered Popcorn." And so they came to Philadelphia, and I remember the gowns they had on. I thought they were terrible. They were so chintzy and cheap-looking. I thought oh, these poor girls!

Singing with my father in [the premier gospel group] the Dixie Hummingbirds, I was accustomed to being onstage in gowns because I was having gowns made from the time I was a kid. The Supremes were wearing red gowns, sort of cheap, fitted in the waist. They weren't bubble dresses, but they kind of ballooned out at the bottom. I remember I saw those dresses around the corner on Columbia Avenue, in one of the stores. And that was the problem for me, that I went, "Hey, that's that dress I saw!" Nobody in the audience recognized it but me.

But despite the dresses, they were great. Of course, at that time my favorite group was Martha and the Vandellas. I thought the Supremes were very good, but Martha and the Vandellas! That was my group! I always wanted to be a Vandella. That was one of my aspirations. I would have loved to sing with the Vandellas. I almost did, too!

Almost like the Beatles-Stones dichotomy a few years later, the Supremes were seen as wholesome, glamorous, and frothy, while Martha and the Vandellas were credited with being funkier and more "authentically" black.

At the time, I thought Martha and the Vandellas were more soulful. And that wasn't unusual for me to think that way because [Berry Gordy] was going for something very different with the Supremes. Let's go into the pop market; why aren't we there? And I think that was brilliant on his part, really. Because that's where the Supremes needed to be. So when he groomed them for that particular genre, I thought it was the best thing he could ever have done. Because we already had the R&B thing down.

Diana was never an R&B act, as it were. She's going to be deemed that, because she's a black person, and unfortunately we still haven't come to grips with the fact that just because you're black doesn't mean you're an R&B artist. You can be a straight-up pop artist, never being able to get into rhythm and blues. I think Hootie and the Blowfish proved that.

Because Florence Ballard had a bigger, bluesier voice than Ross, it's become part of pop culture legend, thanks to the Broadway show **Dreamgirls** *and Mary Wilson's memoirs* [**Dreamgirl: My Life as a Supreme** *and* **Supreme Faith**] *that Florence should have sung lead in the Supremes, and that Diana's elevation to lead singer was unjust.*

I don't know if it was unjust. It's hard to say. I can say this; I believe that what Berry saw in Diana, he didn't see in Flo. And I think it was as simple as that. It may sound trite, but I think he saw it from a marketing standpoint. Flo's voice would have taken them into maybe the top R&B charts and then crossover. But Berry wanted to just go directly for the pop market. And Diana had that uniqueness in her voice; there was no one who sounded like her then, and very few girls who even try now. Diana has her own unique sound. And her look is unique. Berry knew that this was the one different enough to make it. Unfortunately, the idea at that time was one lead singer and two backups, instead of the idea of having two lead singers, or three lead singers, and still have this group. That didn't come about 'til much, much later, in the seventies.

Some of the "Flo can sing, Diana can't" talk came from the musicians. "She still doesn't have a voice!" said one of them, Motown saxophonist and bandleader Thomas "Beans" Bowles, although he softened the remark with an amiable laugh. And added: "Nobody at Motown could sing. But Berry's thing was to get a voice that wasn't easily duplicated. At that time, everybody would copy your record if they had a soundalike. And that would take all the money away. So nobody sounded like Smokey. Nobody sounded like Diana Ross. Nobody sounded like Marvin Gaye."

Detroiter Scherrie Payne, sister of singer Freda Payne ["Band Of Gold"] became a Supreme in 1974. She, too, remembers those red dresses.

—Scherrie Payne—

I sure was a fan of the Supremes. I remember seeing them live a couple of times, at Edgewater Amusement Park [in Detroit] and when they first started to sing, at an affair for our then-governor, G. Mennen Williams. My sister Freda was on the program. This was way before they had any hit records. In fact, they'd just done "Buttered Popcorn," and that's what they sang. They stood out because we were all around the same age group, and they were young black girls—we were the only black people at this affair: me, my parents, Freda, and them. I even remember what they wore, they had these cherry red dresses on. They walked right by my table.

When the Velvelettes came along in the sixties, they always seemed to have a competitive thing going on with the Supremes. The Velvelettes claim to have won at least one of the internal company battle-of-the-bands held at the Graystone Ballroom.

According to the Velvelettes' account, Diana Ross was so furious after going down in defeat to them one time that she was later found in the ladies' room kicking the door of her stall.

Norma Fairhurst says that Esther Gordy Edwards told her that the Supremes had been added to a Velvelettes tour of England only at Motown's insistence.

Both groups were in close quarters during those Dick Clark Caravan of Stars tours. There were teenage shenanigans.

—Mildred Gill Arbor—

We did a Dick Clark tour, and the Supremes were along. And Diane [as she was known] Ross, she had her own little thing, she did. I don't want to say that what happened between her and me was humorous, it just goes to show, everybody has a different kind of personality. The Dick Clark tour was by bus, it was called the Caravan of Stars, and any seat that was in the front of anything belonged to Diane. And she let you know that, either by her appearance there, or if someone else was sitting there, or if something belonging to you was there, it would end up in the back of the bus.

The original Supremes: top, Mary Wilson;
lower left, Diana Ross, and right, Florence Ballard.

We were all kids. When you're teenagers, you do stupid things. But I think some of the things that she did, she did to other people, and it extended over the years. I didn't have a lot of personal contact with her. I had a few conversations with some of the other girls about some of the things that happened with respect to the chaperone, who happened to be her mother. I just wasn't happy with the way she talked to her, or the way she treated her. I thought there should be a little bit more respect, and it sort of shocked me. I was never taught to disrespect my elders, and Diane did that to her mom.

Velvelettes lead singer Carolyn Gill Street and Ross were close, but the rest of the Velvelettes were not big fans of the Supremes.

Well, when we arrived on the scene in Detroit, we were unique because we were all in school, and we were very conservative individuals. We could all sight read, we all played the piano, we all wrote music, so we might have been a bit more advanced than the rest of the female groups. We dressed a little differently because we were in school. They were dressed a little bit more flamboyantly. We were pegged at first as the only group they'd allow to be interviewed because of our vocabulary. I guess we were better educated.

We had very tight harmony, much better than the other ladies. We actually overdubbed, I know, for sure, on one of the Supremes songs, to make the background fuller.

But Diane—she'd hog the mirror; when she'd come into a room, she'd just want to take the whole room over. But I would like to think she's changed, that she's become a lovely adult.

By 1967, Gordy was fed up with what he saw as Florence Ballard's increasingly erratic performances. He

started to cast his net out for a new Supreme. With the
Velvelettes on hiatus, due to marriage and other things,
Norma Barbee was called down to Detroit to try out for
the Supremes.

—Norma Barbee Fairhurst—

Florence and I looked very much alike back then. We
were both light-complected, had a little acne. So I went down,
and actually interviewed, like I was interviewing for a job. I'm
not quite sure who I even spoke with. But Diane and I never
got along, so I knew I would not be picked to take Florence's
place. We both sang first soprano, we both looked alike,
[Florence] was a little heavier-set—reason I mention that is
the wardrobe, I would not be able to fit into Florence's clothing.
And they wanted to offer me a salary, a flat salary, that would
not have paid for my babysitter. It was very minimal, not
much.

My gut feeling was that they wouldn't pick me anyway,
because Diane and I didn't get along.

Diane and Carol [Street, of the Velvelettes] got along
fabulously. They used to share hotel rooms when we'd travel
with the Supremes. So she got to know her quite well.

Cindy Birdsong, of Patti Labelle's Bluebelles, was
brought into the Supremes as Florence Ballard's replacement
in 1967. But when Gordy renamed the group "Diana Ross
and the Supremes," arguing to a protesting Mary Wilson
that the group was now more valuable with "two entities,

Diana Ross and the Supremes," it was apparent that Ross was being groomed for flight from the group.

I can account for the quality of the 1967 model Supremes, whom I saw that summer when my parents took me [and my two younger brothers, in strollers] to the Michigan State Fair, at Woodward and Eight Mile, in Detroit. They were stunning. I remember three shimmering columns of silver, as bright as lasers, as they sang "I Hear A Symphony" and Ross went through a gymkhana of frenetic arm movements.

Nineteen seventy was the year Ross was set to leave the Supremes. At the time, Scherrie Payne was a teacher at the Grayling School of Observation on State Fair, just off Woodward.

—Scherrie Payne—

Someone told me that when Motown was going to replace Diana, when she was going to leave the group and they were trying to come up with a lead singer to replace her, my name was brought up. But someone said, "Oh no, she's not interested in singing. She just wants to teach school." Someone told me that last year, and my heart just sank! Oh! Even though I ended up with the Supremes, I could have been the one; I could have said that I took Diana Ross's place.

But I guess it wasn't meant to be.

It was Jean Terrell who was destined to replace Diana Ross. The sister of boxer Ernie Terrell, the outspoken sing-

er was not as glamour-obsessed as her predecessor. She led the Supremes to several notable hits: "Up the Ladder To The Roof," "Nathan Jones," and "Floy Joy." Then in 1972, Cindy Birdsong became pregnant, and left the group.

Philadelphian Lynda Laurence was living in Detroit, after singing background for Stevie Wonder on his hit "Signed, Sealed, Delivered," and touring behind the song with him. The daughter of Ira Carter, founder of the legendary gospel group the Dixie Hummingbirds, Laurence was a polished and professional singer, a graduate of a Philadelphia charm school who didn't need Motown to teach her how to walk. She had a no-nonsense attitude that Mary Wilson found pushy. But in those early days, when Wilson saw her sing with Wonder, she wanted her in the group.

—Lynda Laurence—

I'd worked with Stevie for two years, and we were performing at an outdoor theater in Washington, D.C. one night when Cindy Birdsong and Mary Wilson came to the show. Cindy knew my sister [Sundray Tucker], because she had replaced Cindy in the Blue Belles. So Cindy's thought immediately was, "Oh, let's get Sundray to replace me because we look alike." My sister was on one side, me on the other. Mary said, "Well, I kind of like the other sister."

I was convinced my sister would get it. I told everybody, "My sister's going to be in the Supremes!" I was all excited and everything. So I was quite happy. About a week or so passed, and [Motown choreographer] Cholly Atkins called me. He said, "Baby, the girls looked at Sundray and they like her, but Mary still wants you to come in." Then it was just me and Mary; I went in and auditioned again. I wasn't going to go, but Stevie said, "Look, with me, you'll be a backup singer. With the Supremes, you'll be a Supreme! It's a whole different thing. So go, at least try it." So I went because Stevie told me to.

I didn't think for one second I'd get it, so I was shocked that I got it. I fit into the gowns—at that time I was a stick. I had to be fitted for them because Cindy was a bit heavier than me. They had gorgeous gowns made just for us, too.

Those shimmering gowns are a big part of the Supremes experience. Mary Wilson wrote in her book Supreme **Faith** *that she didn't know where most of the pre-Cindy Birdsong Supremes dresses were. A few are in the Motown Museum in Detroit; some others are in the collection of Detroit-based clothing archivist Sandy Schrier.*

—Lynda Laurence—

I'd say the gowns were maybe 75 percent of the Supremes experience. Even today, it is extremely important. The clothing is what made this act stand out and be completely different from other acts. The Supremes were known for their costumes as much as they were for their voices, and the music they sang. Obviously, because Diana makes five changes in her show, it's still very important!

I replaced Cindy Birdsong. I am a lead singer, but I wasn't

allowed to sing leads with the Supremes, because the thought at the time was you have a lead, and two girls. I tried to get them to see that times were changing, and these sorts of things need to be put into play, but they just weren't ready for it.

Diana Ross' departure from the Supremes had an immediate, deflating effect on the Supremes. Berry Gordy's attention was now diverted from his former pet group to his striving Galatea, Ross, and her solo career. But Motown's songwriter/producers and its powerful new female executive Suzanne DePasse hadn't given up on the group—not yet.

—Lynda Laurence—

Suzanne DePasse was supportive. The problem was, there were so many transitions going on at the same time. Diana had transitioned into her own career, and Motown was not sure how to handle that. It appeared to us that they were putting most of their eggs in her basket, and we were sort of left out in the cold. I went to Stevie as a good friend and said, "Look, we need a songwriter." So he came up with a song, "Bad Weather." My brother actually wrote the lyrics. So we recorded that, and it probably would have done better here— it did very well in Europe—if they had just put a little more behind it. Some of the producers—Frank Wilson, Smokey Robinson, Stevie—really did try to help out. I think Suzanne was instrumental in getting Jimmy Webb to do an album with us. She was trying to be in our corner.

In 1974, Lynda Laurence left the Supremes to have a baby, and was replaced by her predecessor, Cindy Birdsong. Then lead singer Jean Terrell decided she wanted out, leading to Scherrie Payne's hiring. Payne by then had quit teaching and was recording for Invictus, the label Holland-Dozier-Holland started when they left Motown. Her sister Freda also recorded for Invictus, and Lamont Dozier was Scherrie's boyfriend.

Interestingly enough, before he'd started Motown, Berry Gordy had trained and managed the teenage Freda Payne, and even recorded her, but their mother didn't like the contract he offered.

—Scherrie Payne—

I was probably about twelve or thirteen when Berry managed my sister. Then Berry and my mother clashed over the contract, and so that never was consummated. And I remember, in fact, Freda recorded a song of Berry's called "Father Dear." The B-side was called "Save Me A Star," that was written by Berry and Janie Bradford. It was never released because Freda and my mother didn't sign the contract. He didn't even have Mary Wells then. Freda would have been his first female singer.

Lamont Dozier, who was my boyfriend at the time, had gone to Los Angeles on business, and had gone to a party with Mary Wilson. They were talking and she mentioned that Jean Terrell was leaving the group and they were looking for a new lead singer. So he suggested me.

They talked on Thursday; Mary called me and I flew out that Saturday. Cindy Birdsong picked me up at the airport and we immediately went to Mary's house and started rehearsing because they had an engagement the following Saturday, a week's time. So I had to learn all that material, the steps and everything. We worked tirelessly, into the wee hours of the morning, every night. Our first job was, I think, the Arizona State Fair. Mary said if you can do this, then you can have the position. They were very happy. And I was, too!

The ur-Supreme, Diana Ross, couldn't resist coming 'round to check out the new girl.

—Scherrie Payne—

It was right after I got into the group, and we were rehearsing every day at Mary's house. Diana just happened to stop by. Mary said, "Oh, that's odd, she never comes over to my house! It's because there's a new singer . . . and she wants to see who you are."

She always liked me, though—Diana. She was always nice to me. Regardless of what other people say.

She worked hard. She had a goal, and she didn't let anything get in the way of her goal. She stayed focused. She was a hard worker, I can say that for her. She achieved something so tremendous, way beyond our imagination, and probably hers as well. So I have to take my hat off to her.

Maybe I wouldn't have done it that way, I'm a different type personality, but she's very ambitious and she saw her dream fulfilled. We all make mistakes; we were all maturing and learning. There are some things I've done or said that I've regretted. But I still feel good about myself. I've never really stepped on anyone's toes, or ruined someone or humiliated someone for my own self-aggrandizement.

Maybe she feels the same way, even though people talk about her. I still have to take my hat off to her. She's a great performer, a great entertainer, and she worked her buns off to get where she is.

Ross didn't seem to let anybody intimidate or boss her around. Except maybe, Berry Gordy.

I wish I'd had that input from Berry when I was in the group. That would have made all the difference in the world. That wasn't the case.

Mary Wilson wrote in one of her books that she thought the Supremes line-up of Mary, Cindy, and Scherrie had the most glamour and pizzazz.

Oh yeah, I agree. I loved it when it was me, Mary, and Cindy. And I think we could have done great things if we had just been left alone. Being able to carry on and do like we wanted to do.

Speaking truthfully, I think the problem was Mary's (then-) husband [Pedro Ferrer]. In fact, I know that was the problem. If he had just stayed out of it, we could have really carried on, like the Temptations have carried on all these years, and done some wonderful things. Even in spite of Motown. We could have forced them to generate more interest.

It's almost like Mary Wells' situation, where she was deferring to a husband who wasn't advising her well.

I never could understand it. I could never be like that. That's why it's not good to marry someone in the business. Although most of these men aren't in the business! The women meet them, and all of a sudden, they're in the business and they know more than you.

Diana and Mary have had a particularly embattled, sister-like relationship, culminating in the famous Ross-shoving-Wilson episode during the 1983 Motown 25 TV special. As the story goes, during the taping of the show, as Ross kept moving forward, Wilson kept stepping up behind her so as not to be too far in the background, until Ross became angry and pushed her back into what she saw as the proper place. The shove was cut from the telecast of Motown 25 before it aired.

The later generation Supremes are admirers of Ross.

—Lynda Laurence—

When I was with the group, we were playing the Cocoanut Grove in Los Angeles, and Diana was pregnant with her second child. She came to the show. She said to me, "This is a wonderful profession we're in and everything, and I love

it, but there's nothing more fulfilling than being a mother."
I said, "Well, you know, I'm going to remember that." And I
did. I now know what she means.

*In 1976, Cindy Birdsong departed again, to be replaced
by Susaye Green. By 1978, Wilson, prompted by her husband,
decided to break off from the Supremes and go solo. She
was, as she wrote in her memoir* **Supreme Faith,** *tired
of hiring new Supremes and then having them gang up
against her.*

—Scherrie Payne—

Actually, I didn't leave. Mary decided [to quit] because
Pedro had just talked her into becoming a solo artist. So I
didn't leave; I wanted to continue.

I was just devastated when she said she wanted to go
solo. 'Cause I thought, that's the end of me. But Motown was
going to continue on. Susaye and I were going to find a third
girl, and we did find a third person, my good friend Joyce
Benson Wilson, who was with Tony Orlando and Dawn.
Joyce is from Detroit, too. I'd already talked to Joyce about it, I
introduced her to Susaye, and Susaye loved her. We had told
Motown that was what we wanted.

Next thing we know, an edict was passed down that they
were going to just retire the group. I found out through the
grapevine that Diana had issued that order. If there were going
to be no original members in the group, she wanted it put on
the shelf. She didn't want the Supremes to be an in-and-out

door of people coming and going, which I can understand. I think maybe she felt if there were too many members coming and going, it would take away from it.

So they decided to retire the group, and they were trying to figure out what to do with Susaye and me. We both wanted to be solo artists, but they said there wasn't room on the roster for us both to be solo artists. So we had a meeting up at Berry's house, and they were going to make us into another group, with Syreeta Wright. He was going to call us the Super Group or something, because all of our names started with an "S" —Scherri, Susaye, and Syreeta. And we were all writers. But then Syreeta did that record with Billy Preston, "With You I'm Born Again," and that was a hit. So there went that. She went off in another direction. So they decided to just partner Susaye and I up. And that's what we did, for the *Partners* album.

We never actually got a chance to tour. We did the album, and a couple of guest spots, we did *The Mike Douglas Show*. After that, our contracts got dropped, in '80.

Laurence, Payne, and a new member, Freddie Poole, were touring in the late 1990s as FLOS, "Former Ladies of the Supremes." Cindy Birdsong, Jean Terrell, and Sundray Tucker have also toured as FLOS. In a two-week period in the summer of '97, they gave concerts in London, Sri Lanka, and Coventry, England.

—Lynda Laurence—

When we were in Austria a couple of weeks ago, Diana

was opening there. Her people called and said she was going to try to be at our show. And we were so excited, but then she couldn't because her show and our show started at the same time. We said, "Oh, man," because we were really looking forward to seeing her. I don't in any way have anything negative to say about her. I've seen her on a couple of occasions, and she's always been quite nice to me. I have always given her the proper respect, because she's one of the original—with Mary and Florence—members of the group. And so naturally, you feel very odd, whenever she's around, that she'd even want to come to the show.

I'd love to see all of us back together, to tell you the truth, to do one big show.

A reunion of all generations of Supremes was unlikely, since Mary pressed a lawsuit against the FLOS for using the Supremes' name.

—Scherrie Payne—

As of February of 1996, when I was served, Mary is suing us. But I love her still. She and Freda are good friends, so they've maintained contact. Mary's mother Johnnie Mae Wilson just passed, and I was so sad. I sent Mary a condolence card.

Mary doesn't want us to use the name "Supremes" in any form or fashion. Even saying "formerly of." But Motown owns the name. I've never had a chance to sit down and talk to her. I wish she had called me first before she did this. We could have worked it out.

*From left: Scherrie Payne, Jean Terrell, and Lynda Laurence
toured in the early 1990s as "Former Ladies of the Supremes," or FLOS.*

—*Lynda Laurence*—

We do all the old stuff, everything from "Where Did Our
Love Go?" and "Baby Love"—all of it. You have to. The audience
wouldn't let us get away without it. Then we transition into
Jean's songs, "Up The Ladder To The Roof," "Stoned Love," and
all. And the audience loves it.

I can't believe there's not enough room for all of us out
there. There is.

In fact, the biggest complaint I've heard recently about
Diana's show is that she only does two Supremes songs. We've
almost been following her around Europe; we opened in
England, and she came literally days after we left. She does a

fabulous show, but a lot of people think she's got to add more Supremes things.

I can understand where she's coming from too, because she's been away from the Supremes much longer than she was with them.

In 1999, Diana visited Laurence and Payne backstage at a FLOS show, and complimented them.

—Scherrie Payne—

It really puts the stamp of approval on our group. I appreciated that she felt that it was done in Supremes fashion, because that's what we do. She was very gracious, very kind.

Indeed, Diana called upon Laurence and Payne to join her the following year for her "Return to Love" Supremes tour. Negotiations with Mary broke down, and Ross toured with Laurence and Payne, to less than full houses, and mixed reviews, many of which mentioned Mary's absence.

Both Payne and Laurence admit to mixed feelings about Motown after their experience as Supremes.

—Scherrie Payne—

I wish Motown would have done more for the group. But maybe, if I'd been a different type person I could have made them generate more interest. But I wasn't a pushy type person. I sort of stayed in the background. They were always nice to me. They were never unkind, but I felt that I came in on the tail end, when it was waning, for whatever reason.

—Lynda Laurence—

I have a few hurt feelings about Motown. The company has the potential to go on forever. The music, of course, will go on forever. But they could not make the transition from the old way of thinking. The business changed, but Motown didn't change. And you cannot not change. I saw a lot of artists not get their proper royalty.

It's a shame, because it's a fabulous company, without which a lot of us would not have such careers. I had a lot of support and backing from my family; unfortunately a lot of the artists didn't have that. They'd come through, have one or two hits, then they wouldn't get the proper royalties. And those kinds of things are sad.

My biggest gripe with Motown is that they didn't want the artists to understand the business. They wanted to keep them in the dark and do their creative thing, but not the business. When I came in, I came in with a very high-powered lawyer, because I knew—when I first saw the contract, I said, "Ha!"

Motown was one of the best things to come along in a long time. On the other side of that, there ended up being a lot of problems. Still and all, where would we be without Motown? You have to give it the respect it's due.

Chapter Eight
—Kim Weston—

ONE OF THE MOST alluring voices in Motown's female stable of artists belongs to Kim Weston. It's a shame that she's mostly known today for her estimable duets with Marvin Gaye ("It Takes Two," etc.) because Weston was also one of Motown's most accomplished and subtle ballad singers. But because a ballad singer with deep roots in jazz and blues wasn't going to appeal to a teenaged audience in the sixties, Weston had to content herself with modest success.

Born in 1939, the Detroit native graduated from the city's Miller High School, and at nineteen was singing with the Wright Special, Thomas Wright's gospel group. She was "discovered" by Johnny Thornton, a cousin of Motown's star songwriter/producers, Eddie and Brian Holland. Brought to Motown in 1961 by Thornton, Weston impressed everybody with her voice, if not the songs she'd written. She was offered a contract with Motown, and signed.

Her first record, "Love Me All The Way" was released

in 1964. In 1965, she recorded Holland-Dozier-Holland's "Take Me In Your Arms (Rock Me A Little While)," a song with a pleasant, jazzy rhythm that was later picked up and covered, with Weston's swinging groove intact, by the Doobie Brothers.

Her duets with Gaye were recorded and released toward the end of her stint at Motown, which came to a close in 1967. She left Motown that year along with her husband, A&R chief Mickey Stevenson. Both popped up for a time on MGM Records.

When her marriage to Stevenson ended in the '70s, Weston found a new career in public service. She worked for the city of Detroit, organizing youth arts groups and helping found the Festival of the Arts. After some time in Israel, living with the Black Hebrews, Weston returned to Detroit.

Whether she's had day jobs or not, in sickness or in good health, she mostly kept performing, doing club dates in Detroit and around the country, and appearing in plays. But in recent years Weston has struggled with ill health, which has kept her from performing. As of late winter 2017, she was recovering from surgery in a Detroit area nursing home.

—Mickey Stevenson—

If you're asking me who my best singer was, that would be Kim Weston. Kim had a great voice, an absolutely great gift. It was like steel sometimes. She'd hit certain notes, and it could shatter a house. Great voice, and her spiritual convictions at that time were very strong. So that kind of gave her something to ride on. I think that diminished as she faced more life outside. We hovered over most of our artists, mainly female, to protect them during their time at Motown. But eventually they step out from under your wing and they're out there. All you can hope is that they've got enough of whatever it takes to battle against the elements. And some did not, some did. At that point it's out of your hands.

Weston was signed to Motown as a solo artist in 1961—but that wasn't her first contact with the label.

—Kim Weston—

I'd been singing with a gospel group called The Wright Special. And The Wright Special went to Motown, and that was my first time at Motown; I did a recording there with them. That was before I signed a contract.

I went [alone], it was 1961, and I signed a contract that September. The first part of the year [1962], I started recording. My first song was Norman Whitfield's first song; it was called "It Should Have Been Me." He later did a marvelous job on it with Gladys [Knight]. But they released that, and they released one that Mickey [Stevenson] wrote on me called "Love Me All The Way," so they were back-to-back. But what happened was, deejays in the South liked "Love Me All The Way," and that became my first little hit.

157

I have mixed emotions about Motown, because they were just learning. There were a lot of young people that were experimenting. So there was a lot of trial and error. But it was better than what I was doing before I went there.

Although Kim had some modest success with her singles, it was with Marvin Gaye that she broke out and became one of Motown's better-known singers. Her connection with Gaye started as a touring partnership.

Actually, Marvin and I were traveling together. After I had "Love Me All The Way," and it had a nice bit of exposure, then they started sending me on the road as Marvin's co-star. So we did that for three or four years before we ever recorded together. He was recording with Mary Wells while I was traveling with him; unfortunately, we never did any duets together [while on the road]. Then when Mary Wells left Motown, it was a natural, with me traveling with him, for me to go in the studio with him.

Weston isn't surprised that Wells' career faltered after she left Motown.

Mary was very sweet. Naive, but she and I got along very well. Matter of fact, we shared dressing rooms on most of the shows. But I have to give Motown credit; they really took care of the artists in many ways. Some things they didn't, but as far as protecting the artists on the road, and the bookings and all, they were very good with that.

Weston and Gaye were a natural pair, their voices blending with a certain innocence he didn't achieve with any other female singing partner. Today, Weston believes that she knew a different man than the one who fled to Belgium in the late seventies.

You know, the Marvin that I worked with is not the Marvin that everybody said he turned out to be. I really didn't get to know that person, and I'm glad. He was a very shy person when I knew him, very gentle, very sweet and concerned, and very protective of me. And he was a perfect gentleman! Which I later heard, he was just the opposite. It's unfortunate.

My personal views are that the things that you have to go through contribute a lot to what happens to a person. We all went through a lot, and being an artist, and someone who's creative, like Marvin, it's even harder.

Kim Weston in a Motown publicity shot.

For instance, during the time I was at Motown, the artists weren't allowed to produce themselves. And if they wrote a song, they had to give a person a part of it, in order to get it recorded. Those sort of things, even though you follow it, it still has an effect on you.

Marvin and I worked very well together. As a matter of fact, I got to be fairly close to his family. He was really like a brother to me. And when I left Motown, the biggest problem that I had was leaving the artists. I don't feel that I was treated right artistically . . . because the life of a record during that time was three months, and any time an artist had a hit, within three months before they stopped playing that record, the next one would be out. But many times it would be six to nine months before I had a new record out, even if I had a hit.

I don't know if it was because my husband was A&R director, or what, but . . . that's one of the reasons that when he said he was going to leave, I thought it would be better for me to leave, too.

For most of her stay at Motown, Weston was either going with Mickey Stevenson or married to him. While a romantic attachment with Motown's top boss may have helped Diana Ross, Weston isn't so sure her link with Stevenson helped. And when she disagreed with him in the studio, as her producer, their romantic status made it all the more difficult.

There was a thing, not just with Mickey, but with all the producers, when they wanted you to sing something a certain way, it didn't leave room for your creativity. And if you're the singer, you're supposed to be able to input something into whatever it is you're singing; that's one of the things that happened with Marvin. With all that creativity, he did not need anyone telling him how to sing a song!

So a lot of times Mickey and I would clash on how he heard a song, the interpretation, and how I heard it. And unfortunately, "My Baby Loves Me" was the biggest problem, because he gave that to Martha [Reeves] and she sung it just like I did! That was our biggest clash. She sung it just like me, and I give her credit, my sister, she admits that she did. She didn't see any way else to do the song. And by that time, Mickey had forgotten whatever it is he'd wanted me to do.

Stevenson claims that "Dancing In The Street" was originally supposed to be for Weston.

He did? Well . . . I don't know if it was supposed to be for me, but I told him I wanted it! Because he and Marvin and Ivy Hunter were writing it in the attic of our house. And when I heard it, I ran upstairs and said, "Whose is that?" And I guess because Martha had the hit on "My Baby Loves Me," [Martha] got it. But maybe it was scheduled for me. "My Baby Loves Me" was mine, but because he took it and gave it to her, she had the hit on it . . . so her next record was "Dancing In The Street."

So it was for me? Mickey never admitted that to me, I must tell you.

Stevenson claimed Weston wasn't angry that he gave the song to Martha Reeves because "she [Kim Weston] had me."
Weston erupts.

Oh no! He didn't say that! That's a lot of nerve!

"Just Loving You" and "Thrill A Moment" were my favorites of the songs I did. For one thing, I'm a ballad singer, and I think "Just Loving You" was one of the prettiest ballads. That was just my second release. Johnny Allen did a marvelous arrangement on it, and it wasn't in the traditional Motown style. It was in a blues/jazz style, and it's still one of my favorite songs. But it was definitely the favorite of the songs I did at Motown. "Thrill A Moment" is next because it was so different and light.

While the Supremes got most of Berry Gordy's attention, Weston doesn't hold too much of a grudge.

They did, but one thing that I do remember is that who-ever was hot got Mr. Gordy's attention. So when somebody else was hot, they got his attention. It just so happens that I never really got hot enough to get his attention! *In that way.* Because I never had the smash, smash record. But there have been many times that he walked up and said things to me.

I remember once we were at the Fox Theatre, doing the Motown Revue, and he walked up to me and said, "Kim, you're making my stars look bad." I didn't exactly know how to take that! 'Cause I'd signed away seven years of my life. But I think that was his way of complimenting me.

Weston never stopped performing over the years, but her health had deteriorated to the point where she sought help in Israel, in the 1990s.

I was having a lot of problems, and I came here [to Israel] because of my physical problems. I couldn't keep anything in my stomach, and my nerves were just balled up in a knot. I came here to see some specialists, and after they gave me some intense therapy, then they recommended that I go to Danoma with the Black Hebrews, who have a vegan diet, no animal products at all. Between the diet, and the vitamins, exercises . . . it's part of their lifestyle that you exercise every other day. It's a must. They call it "holy concern." So between that, and the love that the people gave me, I'm really doing great. And I thank God, because at one point there, I was just about out of it.

They say it's not a religion, but a way of life. They say they're Hebrews, and they practice a way of life from the Old Testament, which goes with the diet and the whole bit. But it's not considered religious.

I'm now up north of the Sea of Galilee. I'm singing in a restaurant called the Memphis Club. The owner was born here, but he loves Elvis Presley. Every picture that Elvis ever took, he's got all the stamps, all over the wall.

They're taking very good care of me here. This week

there's an art festival going on, they have artists living here, and they have exhibitions where they live. It's like an artists' colony. So I fit right in. One of the few black faces, but don't nobody stare at me.

Chapter Nine
—Brenda Holloway—

BRENDA HOLLOWAY'S RECORDS OFFER some of the most distinctive sounds in the Motown catalog. And no wonder: The Los Angeles native recorded most of her Motown works in her home city, without the ministrations of the Funk Brothers to give her tracks that familiar Motown heft. Instead, producer Hal Davis surrounded her voice with a lighter, jazzier West Coast sound.

Holloway was born in Atascadero, in northern California, and was named after Brenda Starr, the girl reporter in the Sunday comics section of the newspaper.

As a toddler she moved to Watts, in south central Los Angeles, with her mother, sister, and brother. By the time she was a teenager she was studying string performance at the University of Southern California Conservatory of Music, while singing on sessions for Barry White and the Whispers on the side.

In 1964 Holloway impressed Berry Gordy with more than just her vocal talent when she auditioned for him at a Los Angeles disc jockey convention. The seventeen-year-old was wearing a gold pantsuit that might as well have been painted on, set off by gold high heels and a headband; an outfit way beyond her years that went down in Motown history and established her as one of the label's sharpest dressers. (For years her tiny blue beaded minidress was a highlight of the second floor tour at the Motown Historical Museum at 2648 W. Grand Boulevard.) Between her singing and the gold outfit, Gordy signed her immediately, and her biggest hit "Every Little Bit Hurts," recorded in Los Angeles, followed soon afterward.

Holloway was the first West Coast artist signed to Motown, but her distance from Detroit worked against her, she believes, because the home-grown talent grabbed the best Holland-Dozier-Holland and Smokey Robinson songs. But Holloway's signing led to the opening of Motown's West Coast office, to top Motown stars booking L.A. recording sessions, and the eventual wholesale move of the company to California.

Upset by what she saw as a lack of access to songs, Holloway wrote a letter asking Berry Gordy for a release from her contract in 1967.

She was also one of the few Motown divas who wrote songs; her "You've Made Me So Very Happy" was a smash for Blood, Sweat & Tears in 1971, and her song "Ba Ba Ba" ended up on the Supremes' Reflections album. In 1997, at the time of this interview, Holloway was divorced, with four daughters, and living in Los Angeles.

—Brenda Holloway—

I first recorded when I was a teenager, when I was sixteen or seventeen. I did some work with Barry White, and on the Del-Fi label, the Donna label with my sister Patrice Holloway. Patrice had a hit when she was twelve called "The Del-Viking." It was a dance. And I used to go and do the dancing, 'cause she was kind of chunky at twelve, and I was the dancer, so I would dance. She didn't want to dance. She liked to eat, and she was fat.

Then I met Hal Davis with a woman called Patricia Hunt; she's dead now, but she went to school with me, and she introduced me to Hal. And then Mark Gordon and Hal were partners.

Brenda Holloway in the mid-sixties; the brash teenager who
"dressed like a grown lady" to impress Berry Gordy Jr.

My sister was already going, and we used to do a lot of background for a lot of people, Johnny Rivers, Tina Turner, the Blossoms, and the Honeycombs, which was a local studio group, and Darlene Wright [later, Darlene Love]. Before I got started, I used to make my money from singing background.

And then when Hal came out we formed a group with some girls, 'cause I was raised in Watts, which is considered south central Los Angeles, or the ghetto. But I always lived in a home, I didn't live in the projects or anything. So we formed a group with five girls from Watts. I was the sixth, and we were called the Wattesians, and we started doing record hops. Record hops would be held at the high school campuses. They would introduce us, play our record, then have a dance; we'd sing our record.

But there was a life-changing meeting with Berry Gordy, Jr., in Holloway's future. She was a Motown fan and listened to Mary Wells songs while scrubbing the floor. She would tell friends, "I'm going to record for Motown someday." And they'd laugh.

Hal Davis told me that he knew Berry Gordy through one of his friends, Jack Askew, who was working along with Berry, and they were here for a disc jockey convention in '64 at the Cocoanut Grove. So Hal set up an appointment.

And as everybody knows, I got dressed up [*laughs*] like a grown lady, at seventeen, in a real, *real* tight gold pantsuit, with a gold headband and gold heels—that famous Brenda Holloway shape—I went up there and I was singing for hours and hours and hours. I was singing "My Guy" because I didn't have a record out. And these men came into the room, and then they left. And then another man came into the room, and I said, "You know, I'm tired, I've been singing for hours, and I'm supposed to be meeting Berry Gordy. I'm getting ready to leave because I'm tired and I've been singing since about nine o'clock this morning." And it was four. He left the room, and came back with the other men, and he said, "I'm Berry Gordy." I said, "Huh?" He said, "I'm Berry Gordy." I said, "No, you're not!"

Because I'd been complaining to him. And he said, "Yes, I like what I see, I like you, I like your voice, and I want to sign you up. But you have to graduate first." So I called my mother in Watts, I said, "You better put on the best thing you've got, we're going to come pick you up, and honey, you'd better sign this contract because I want to get out of Watts and I can sing for Motown!" And my mother said, "Okay," and they went and picked her up, and I went, and we signed that day.

It took a while for Holloway's everyday life as a Los Angeles teenager to catch up with her newfound status as a Motown pop star.

I was going to college, [majoring] in music, and I was cleaning up the house one night, getting ready for school the next day, and I started mopping the floor. And all of a sudden I heard "Every Little Bit Hurts" [on the radio], and I got so nervous, I said, "Oh, no!" The record's out, and instead of saying "Oh, yes!" I said, "Oh, my God! I'm *scaaared*." But I was happy and excited. I had a record out, but I didn't tell anyone at school.

Then the record got more popular and more popular, and some of the kids at school said, "What's your name?" I said, "Brenda." They said, "Your name Brenda Holloway?" I said, "Mmm hmm." They said, "Honey, what are you here for, you have a hit out!" I said, "I do?"

But soon Motown sent Holloway out on the road, both on Motown Revues and on many of the package tours of the time. She hadn't yet become the typical, polished Motown performer.

I went on the road, to the Uptown [in Philadelphia] with Gladys Knight, Patti LaBelle and the Blue Belles, Jerry Butler, and it was so funny, because I was so nervous, I was doing things like walking diagonally across the stage. And they would throw tomatoes at me and say, "Get off the stage! She can't even walk!"

So Berry got wind of it, and I was walking backstage, in between shows, with a book on my head, so they sent me to charm school, in Los Angeles, to Patricia Stevens School of Modeling and Finishing. After that I was able to get in and out of a car, know what fork to eat with, how to sit, how to stand . . . and I was happy. I had confidence.

Holloway's songs weren't typical Motown because she was a Los Angeles artist recording in Los Angeles.

I was eighteen when "Every Little Bit Hurts" came out. I cut the record out in L.A., and it was really a good, good thing, because our problem, we were trying to imitate the Motown sound, and we had come up with a new, brisk, crossover pop type of Motown sound, with not as much bass, and not as much soul, but it had our own sound. It had the crispness of L.A., and it had the soul of Motown, and it was different. So it was an infusion of the Motown in Detroit and the Motown in L.A.

And so after we got such a good sound and a fresh sound that was crossing over, they would send their artists out here to record. And they opened up the office, because I was their first artist out here. Their first West Coast office, and Stevie would come out, and Marvin . . . so it was really exciting.

Holloway always felt like a Motown outsider. She looks at her Motown colleagues and recalls how much she'd idol-ized them while growing up.

From a little girl, ever since I heard the first Motown record, I would always tell everybody, "I'm going to get on Motown." They'd say, "Yeah, you're crazy." I said, "No, I'm going to get on Motown." They said, "Well, yeah, but you don't even know where Motown is. You know where 103rd Street is, your school and all that." I said, "Well, I'm getting on Motown," and it came to pass.

My favorite Motown artist was Diana Ross. I liked her sound and I liked her uniqueness, although it changed after she got her string of hits; she got more commercial. She reminded me of Eartha Kitt, vocally. What she did in dance, Diana Ross did in music. And very unique; it was sort of a tribal mix of a Caribbean-type voice. She was very different when she first started. After I got there and was using diction, then she started studying my tracks, and then because Berry insisted that she pronounce all her words, she did.

Holloway's image was so different, she found that some thought she was white. It caused some amusing situations on the road.

Well, I was born pronouncing my words; I don't know why. And people would always think I was white on the phone.

As a matter of fact, I have a long nose. When I went on the road, and we would have black and white pictures, people would say, "Brenda Holloway is white." And I'd say, "Oh, I don't think so! Brenda Holloway is black."

I'll never forget it, there was a crowd of white girls behind me, and we were doing a show. And they said, "Well, who are you?" I said, "I'm Brenda Holloway." They said, "No, you're not, Brenda Holloway is white." I said, "No, Brenda Holloway has a long nose, and in black and white pictures, she photographs white. But she's black."

"Oh, no, she's not!" Okay!

They'd always call me the black Barbra Streisand—wish I had her money! But that's been my trademark, my nose, and my vocal stylings, because I have a lot of tribal moans and groans, that are just . . . they show up in my singing, and a lot of times I sing out of my sadness. I try to make happy songs when I'm sad, and sad songs when I'm happy.

That's how I wrote "You've Made Me So Very Happy." I was very sad, and I said, "I'm not going to even go there. I'm going to write a happy song to get myself out of this mood." And I did. And it paid off. But there again, women were not writing songs that much in the sixties; they were not liberated at that time. And I had a fight over the way I wanted it put out. Berry put it out the way he wanted it out.

But then Blood, Sweat and Tears put it out the way I had imagined it, and wanted it to be constructed and put out. And it proved to be a standard.

In the mid-'60s Holloway was one of the few acts chosen to tour with the Beatles.

Opening for the Beatles was the most fantastic, beautiful, educational, historical event of my life. Apart from having my babies. Because they were my idols, next to Diana Ross and Stevie, and the Miracles. Of course, everyone at Motown I loved, but Diana, I singled her out because she was very unique with her sound. And Mary Wells was just a household word. No one could top her in my book.

But traveling with the Beatles was very, very exciting, the highlight of my life in the sixties. They were the most beautiful men. They were so focused, and together, so clean-cut and so "business." They were refreshing. I toured with them on their first United States tour. We went to every state in the United States. We had a plane, their own private jet. They were nice, they were cordial, they were again, business. They were unbelievable. When I say "unbelievable," it's like, you have a doll that comes alive. And you don't want to tell anybody, 'cause they're not going to believe you. It's like, "They're real, and they're with me." But don't tell nobody now, 'cause they'll think you're lying.

Surely, with those four guys out on the road, considering their passion for all things Motown, one of them must have tried something.

One of them tried. In that roundabout way. Ringo . . . but he did it where he couldn't really be caught. He came to my room; it could have been all publicity, I don't know. But he could have gone to anyone's room . . . and he asked me for my hairdryer. And I said, "Okay." And it was in the newspaper the next day.

But I think their music was really their girlfriend. If you've ever been around Stevie Wonder or the Beatles, you know what true genius is, and you do not want to infringe upon that. You want them to be happy, you don't want to tamper, you know, with things that are almost perfect. We don't want to mess with that; we want them to be able to create because they were born to do that. And when you find out what you're born to do, you do that.

Can you imagine me ever kissing a Beatle? Oh, no, I don't think so. I'd probably go, "I can't wash my lips ever."

But they idolized Motown singers, especially the girl singers.

Yes, they did, because Motown was an era, an epoch, something that will never happen again. It was a once-in-a-lifetime thing, as the Beatles were.

A frustrated Holloway wrote a letter to Gordy in 1967 asking for her release from her Motown contract. In the letter she expressed her great admiration for the boss, along with her growing impatience with the offhand way she'd been treated.

I think I'd been there for about three years when I wrote that letter. My dispute and my displeasure was logistically and geographically. I was not able to get to the songs before the other artists got there. Because I had to fly for hours, and they were already back east, they could just drive and get there. And the songs that were being produced for me, if Gladys was in, or Diana was in, or if Mary was in town, well . . . we're waiting on Brenda to come in, but since you're here, come on into the studio. Then I'd get there, and they'd have to start writing all over again.

And it was frustrating, because when you're young, you don't have patience. And you want it now, and you don't want to wait. You become frustrated, and when that happens it's bad. I couldn't deal with it, and that was my problem.

A lot of promises that were made; I didn't want to wait. I saw everyone else making hits . . . and we were children, we were eighteen, but we were not grown. We just came from high school into the Motown stable, into adulthood, and we couldn't make that transition that easily. I made the transition from high school to the Uptown Theater. I had to catch up with what I was doing, competing with people who were bigger than life.

You're a new artist, you're established, but how do you compete with a Gladys Knight, who's been out there performing all her life? You're the new kid on the block; you have to prove yourself. How are you going to prove yourself if you don't have songs out? So that was my frustration.

I always liken myself to the adopted child of Berry's. Because he came, and he hand-picked me. And he wanted me. He didn't really have to have me. But I was hand-picked, and as far as being part of the family, I was adopted and wanted. And I didn't come there broke or looking broke. I wasn't from the projects. I was refined; I've always been refined.

Brenda Holloway in the 1990s. (Courtesy of Bill Baran)

And Berry would say, "You know what to do, you know what to say." Well, all I knew was classical stuff, being focused and regimented and on a schedule. Going out and partying, I didn't believe in that, because I knew I had to get up the next day.

When I was cranky, Berry would say, "Just stay in your room." Just like a little kid! We would be in the hotel and he'd say, "If you're not going to be happy, just stay in your room all day." And I'd say, "Ah shoot, forget him." I'd get mad, then I'd go in, stay for one day, two days, then I'd be depressed again. But he loved me. He wanted me on that label. He enjoyed my singing. He enjoyed me as an artist.

Holloway believed that Diana Ross was taking tales back to Motown and Gordy about what went on while the artists were on the road.

My idol, Diane, was a little bit finicky—I'm not going to say jealous—but she was finicky, and she would start trouble. She would go back and tattle; she'd tell little white lies on me. She'd tell that I'd been out all night partying, and that I'd been with this man or . . . just little white lies. And I'd say, "You little . . . you little bone!" I'd say, "Oh, I don't think so!" I'd tell my mother 'cause I would never want to fuss. They were like my sisters, and they were people that I respected. But I'd say, "How could that little bone tell that lie on me? I'm going to just blow on her and knock her down!"

And my mother'd say, "That little . . . she's just something else." Diane would sometimes treat her mom bad on the road, and her mom would say, "Look, I don't have to stay out here. I can just go home."

And on the road she'd be like *la la la la la la*, singing all night, and we'd have to yell, "We're sick! Could you *shut up*? The show's over!"

But you know, I look at her and I say, Diana Ross, she created that person, and she was the best person to do Diana Ross. She never got tired of herself. She loved herself! Even though her voice was squeaky, after a while, she was still singing! You just had to know, if she's not going to be a star, she's going to go crazy.

So, okay. Just let her do what she wants to do. Because I never paid her that much attention. I loved Diane. I thought she was so beautiful, but I said, "Deep down, she's just a witch. She's just trying to get everybody out of the way so she could be the one!" So I took her as a joke.

There was one time, out on a package show, that Holloway says she took defensive action against her idol.

One time, it was some show, and I had my own hairspray. You know we had those beehive wigs in those days, and if you didn't spray those jokers, they would fall. And you'd have a big old mess; you could have some flies up there, or anything! And we were backstage, and I was always quiet, I'd think, "Just let me keep my mouth shut, because I am the adopted child of Motown."

And these girls had been on the road for a long time, and I'm just coming out fresh, and I have all these clothes, I have everything, right? They're looking at me like, well, who is she? So anyway, Diane said, "Well, this is my hairspray." I said, "I don't think so!" She said, "Oh, yes it is." So Shirley of the Shirelles said, "Diane, that is not your hairspray, okay?" And then Mary [Wilson], she always went along with Diane, she got in it. "Well, you just better chill out, girlfriend, because we can roll before the show, you know, like rock and roll?"

And I didn't say anything because I didn't want Diane to go lie on me and say I'd been back here fighting. If anybody's going to fight, let the Shirelles and the Supremes fight. I'm not going to be in it!

I said, "Oh, forget about it," but [the Shirelles] said, "No, we're not going to let her get away with that." So they got the hairspray from her. She'd just come in and take over, as little as she was! And all I had to do was just go sit on her with one leg, and she would not be able to sing for a few days!

She had a lot of nerve, but that's Diane Ross. You'd have to respect it because she was the one making the hits. One time, when I put out my second record, they pulled mine in, because we were a small company, and [the Supremes' song], which was "Where Did Our Love Go," was becoming a hit, and they pulled mine in! And I was frustrated, I was so upset, because it was a good song, but it was a conflict in sales.

As much as she loved the company, after a while she felt there was too big a gap between Gordy's promises and the reality of her career in Los Angeles.

Berry always let us know, we are a family, and Brenda,

you are going to have your turn, you're going to be in Vegas. He wanted me to be in Vegas, but I just couldn't see it when everybody else was getting hits, and I was saying, "When am I going to record? Where are my songs?"

As a matter of fact, I left Motown in the middle of a session with Smokey Robinson. I just couldn't take it anymore. I just had one song to do, and I was there for a few weeks, waiting on them to finish. Then when the other artist came in, they would just say, "We're outta here, so give us this material." They didn't know it was my song. But I felt it was a breach of my contract, and the only way I could make them know that I was really frustrated was to really just leave. I wrote Berry a letter, because I loved Mr. Berry Gordy. Because as I said, I was just mopping my kitchen and going to school before I met him.

Glamour was always a big part of the Brenda Holloway mystique. Her blue minidress, on display at the Motown Historical Museum in Detroit, is a tour-stopper.

Oh, they have my little glittery dress at the Motown Museum, yes. Did you like my little dress? That was from the garment district. My mother was the one who did wardrobe; she shopped for everybody, which was her pleasure. She was born in September, so she was a perfectionist. She'd say, "You can be naked, but just have some stockings on!"

I never thought that I was pretty because I had unusual features for a black person. It was always, "why is your nose so long?" and "why do you have freckles?" They would call me Pickle Nose, and that would really disturb me. So I'd find out their bad qualities and get into a fight. My family, my brother would always go, "Hi, Pickle Nose!"

This business is fast. What was so devastating to me wasn't the beauty and glamour of performing, but all the stuff backstage. You have to be very strong and always have to have your guard up, and that's why I'm into young people and education, because you always have to have someplace to go or something to do when you don't have a hit.

Because hits are not guaranteed, and the public is fickle, sometimes they don't like you for a period of time. Looking at it from my standpoint now, I would encourage and admonish young people to get some kind of trade, or get some degree, so they'll have something to fall back on, and they won't be frustrated and idle during the time when there's a lull in their career.

Both before and after her Motown stint, Holloway has done many backup sessions. In the later '60s she did several notable ones with Joe Cocker.

I met Joe when he first came out here [in 1969]. Merry Clayton—Baby Sister—she introduced me to him, and we went into the studio. He came right off the plane, and we went into the studio the day he came, and one of the songs we sang with him is used on [TV's] *The Wonder Years*, and I'm still getting residuals from that to this day. He is another one who's a genius. Wild was not the word; [Joe] was out of his brain! He was sweet, very nice. But totally gone.

My sister [Patrice] didn't tour with us, but she sang with us. She was so gorgeous, a typical black kind of beauty, the little round nose, the little round face, the voluptuous type of figure, not skinny or anything. She worked with Cheryl Ladd [then known as Cherie Moor] in the group Josie and the Pussycats. And she toured with Wayne Newton. She worked in Vegas a lot. Sister was more of a business type person than I was. I'm more of an artist. I like real estate, stuff I can see.

I was able to concentrate on my singing. I didn't have a real man in my life in those days. Because I was regimented, I was a concert musician. I wasn't into trying to get a relationship. I knew if I got involved in anything else but my music it would be trouble. I didn't even fool with dolls or anything. I didn't understand why [other female artists] were having men troubles and why they were married.

People who live in the ghetto, they want to drink and do drugs. They don't know that there's a whole world outside of the ghetto. Then they get locked in and they can't get out. It's just a scenario I'm using, but I didn't get involved in the things that were going on. I said I can go here, or I can go to the bottom, or I can go to the top. I knew that it was my ticket out of the ghetto, my talent. I didn't have to have a man to complete me. I didn't have to have a man to validate me. I had Brenda. From a little girl, my mother said, "If your hair's done and your shoes look good, it doesn't matter what's in between. It can be cheap."

My mother was mixed, and very fair-skinned, and she never called us black or used the word nigger or Negro in our house. I didn't know I was black, for a long, long time. But then I went down South, and they said, "You might talk like a white girl, but baby, you are black, okay?" And they said, "You are a nigger."

I said, "Wait a minute, Mama?" And she said, "Look in the mirror, baby, because you are black, but you're not a nigger." I said, "Okay, that's fine." She just said, "You're as good as anyone. You get out there and make it." She was a pusher. She'd say, "You get out there and perfect that talent." So I didn't need anyone to validate me. I needed my mom to push me.

Brenda did get married in 1970, to a minister.

I was very unhappy in my marriage. I couldn't make a decision. I didn't feel I could pick my own clothes. By being an entertainer, you lose so much of the normal way of life because you're right out there in the public, and you want to be accepted. It's an obsession to please and to know that you're the one who the public wants. That's where my problems would surface, in not choosing my own clothes. Took me a long time to say accept what you do for yourself, and love yourself. I wanted total acceptance from everybody, not just my public. That was a flaw in my personality. I got out of it, with a lot of practice. Not therapy, just practice. I got married to really break that tie from my mom, that dominance. I made a bad decision, to get married, not for love.

I have learned how to deal with church and be balanced in my life. 'Cause I was on the verge of, not being a fanatic, but you're too scared to do anything—God is going to be mad at me if I . . . but God wants you to be happy; God is a god of order. And I had to go through a lot, a very unhappy marriage for eighteen years, to realize that God didn't want me to be unhappy. He wasn't my husband. He was not the one.

In recent years, Holloway found a happier relationship with a Los Angeles teacher.

Jerome Richardson—he was instrumental in me getting back, because when he first met me, he saw something in me. Because I was like 225 pounds when he met me, and I lost ten dress sizes, I went from a 20 to a 10. And he told me, "You are the greatest, you get out on that track and you work." 'Cause he's very positive. He said, "You do this and you do that, because you're Brenda Holloway."

I was saying, "I'm a grandmother, I'm just going to eat and watch babies." He said, "I don't think so, honey. This dormant talent, you still have a lot of life." Losing all this weight, it's been another big transition, but he has walked me through, and he has been there for me. Now we have a lot of spats because he's very domineering too. He's a schoolteacher, and he's a leader, and he deals with kids. He's able to sit down and talk to me, and plan a course, and help me stay focused, and still love me and be nice, and I never found that quality in any other man.

He's the one who said, "Oh, you're going to sing again."

Chapter Ten
—The Velvelettes—

IF MARY WELLS WAS every teenage boy's understanding sweetheart and the Supremes were the untouchable, preening dream goddesses, the Velvelettes were the archetypal early sixties college girls: wholesome, likable, and cute.

The outstate Michigan-based group consisted of a pair of sisters, a pair of cousins, and a friend, all firmly under the thumb of stern parents who insisted upon steering them back to their studies no matter what glitzy distractions Detroit and that flesh palace Motown Records were offering.

Intriguingly enough, Mickey Stevenson, who co-wrote their biggest hit, "Needle In A Haystack," believes that the Velvelettes' roots in Flint (69 miles north of Detroit) and Kalamazoo (140 miles west) gave them more street smarts than the Detroit girl groups. "Flint was a rough place back then," Stevenson notes. "You had to know how to take care of yourself."

Tough or girlish as they were, musically the Velvelettes were the embodiment of girl group vivaciousness, and their string of hits was vibrant if short-lived, including 1964's

"Needle In A Haystack," and the follow-up "(He Was) Really Saying Something" (later a hit for England's Bananarama), which did better with R&B and local Detroit audiences than on the national pop charts.

Their parents' vigilance paid off; each of the four remaining Velvelettes in the late 1990s had a "straight gig" in the professional world. Bertha Barbee McNeal taught music and conducted the choir at Milwood Middle School in Kalamazoo, Mildred Gill Arbor was a third shift surgical nurse at Flint's McLaren Hospital, Carolyn Gill Street was a human resources specialist at Upjohn in Kalamazoo, and Norma Barbee Fairhurst a sales director for the Radisson Hotel in Flint. All of the women were divorced, which is partly why they were able to re-form.

For, unlike some of their more famous Motown siblings, since 1984 [and, as of 2017, still] the Velvelettes have been out there gigging, and with all original members no less (save Betty Kelley, who went on, with everybody's blessing, to become a Vandella). Herewith, a partial Velveletiad:

—Bertha Barbee McNeal—

Norma [Barbee Fairhurst] is my first cousin. Her dad and my dad are brothers. We were in a group in Flint called the Barbees, which is my maiden name and her maiden name. My uncle, her dad's younger brother, has a really nice voice, and he'd started a group. He was the lead singer, and he wanted background voices; we were fourteen, thirteen and twelve—including another cousin by marriage, Joyce.

So there was three of us in the background, and my uncle. Believe it or not, we became known in Flint for singing pop tunes.

One day [in 1957], we got a chance to cut a record. I remember my uncle said it was going to be with some musicians from Detroit. Mickey Stevenson was our producer for this record, which was called "Que Pasa"; the other side was called "The Wind," written by my uncle. I sure wish somebody could find a copy of it; I'd love to have it. Mickey at that time was a struggling producer, very young, and he was telling us he knew a man who was a composer by the name of Berry Gordy. My uncle knew Berry, too. Norma and I didn't know that we were going to hook up with him later. The record did fairly well.

The Velvelettes in 1961. Left to right: Mildred Gill Arbor, Norma Barbee Fairhurst, Carolyn "Cal" Gill Street, Betty Kelley, Bertha Barbee McNeal.

Later, when I decided I wanted to go to college, to Western [Western Michigan University, in Kalamazoo] and major in music, the group broke up. I could play the piano. I'd studied classical piano since I was nine, then [when] I was in the pop group, I started picking up on some rock chords.

One day I went to the student center and saw a beautiful grand piano. I sat down and started playing my Barbees rock songs. Some of the girls gathered around—back then rock was still fairly new, and here you're in an institution of higher learning, and I'm playing rock—that was like, "*Ooo*, cool!" So some of the girls said, "Why don't we start a group?" I said, "Shoot, yeah." That's how Cal comes up with the I'm-the-founder-of-the-group thing. I don't know if I qualify.

—*Carolyn "Cal" Gill Street*—

I was only in ninth grade then, so my sister took me up to Western with her, and Bertha played the piano and I sang, because I knew all the lead parts to any song she played, because I used to sit up under the radio and listen to the music from a station that we used to get from Tennessee. Randy was the deejay; I'm not sure what the call letters were for the station.*

I knew all the other pop/rock that was playing on the local stations, too. But I had to be careful around the house with my father, who was a preacher. He didn't allow us to listen to that kind of music when he was around. We'd sneak around and listen to it when he was asleep. And when he'd work nights.

*Actually, the disc jockey Cal refers to was John R., and the station was Nashville's WLAC. The show's sponsor

was Randy's Record Shop, and it influenced a generation of musicians, including Bob Seger, Mitch Ryder, and Johnny Winter.

—Bertha Barbee McNeal—

So we had probably about ten, twelve girls, and we would just sing some of the songs that were out, and I'd play, at the sock hops. Girls back then wore socks and tennis shoes. We did this for a few months, then there was an African-American fraternity called the Alpha Phi Alphas. They were getting ready to have their talent show. They were offering twenty-five dollars. We could use that money, so we decided to try.

So Mildred and I—I don't know how to say this nicely—we dismissed some of the girls, because I said, "Mildred, I have this cousin in Flint who sings really well, and really high, just like a bird"—and Norma does, she has a high soprano voice. And Mildred said, "I have a sister, Cal, who's really good too, and she has a friend, Betty Kelley, who can sing." So we dismissed the other girls and called them in.

This is how the embryonic Velvelettes were formed. Norma would catch the Greyhound bus up from Flint, on the weekends, and come up. And they'd stay in my dorm; we still have a picture of us in my dorm. We'd practice in the music department, in one of those little rooms, cutting a rug on something like "Money," just doing our thing.

By Jove, if we didn't win first place in that talent show. We got that twenty-five dollars. One of the songs we really loved was "Money." That was one of our first tunes. We did a lot of Impressions tunes, too. We got our outfits at Penney's and Sears; sleeveless, straight black dresses with gloves that came up over the elbows. We didn't have wigs, just our own hair, no extra makeup—we didn't know how. We had this little deal worked out where I would go up to the piano and take off the gloves, one finger at a time, to be cool. We had it worked out, a little routine.

Esther [Gordy Edwards]'s son [Robert Bullock] had seen us at some of the sock hops. He suggested we come to Motown and audition for his uncle, Berry Gordy. We listened to that. We said, "Oh, please!" We had no thoughts of recording. You're young, you have your whole life in front of you. Finally, Cal and Mildred's father, the preacher, he said, "Hey, I'll drive you girls to Detroit one Saturday." So we said, "Hey, what do we have to lose?" So we all jumped in the car and we went to audition on a Saturday.

—Mildred Gill Arbor—

All we really wanted to do was make a record. My father wasn't that enthused. Him being a minister, that was just not what he thought our personal choices should be. It took quite a lot of persuasion to get him to let me and my sister be involved in this rock and roll scene.

—Bertha Barbee McNeal—

Later on, I remember having tears in my eyes, because

this gal, this secretary at Motown was chewing her gum and saying,"I'm sorry, we don't have auditions on Saturdays." We'd come all the way from Kalamazoo, in the winter. We were about to go out the door; fate is unreal. And that recording studio door opened, and who should come out but Mickey Stevenson. He recognized Norma and me. He said, "What are you girls doing here?" He looked at that girl behind the desk and said, "Hey, let them in!"

The Velvelettes were different because they were from "outstate," Flint and Kalamazoo; but they were also set off from the other Motown stars by the fact that they were college girls. Motown offered an earthier curriculum.

None of the groups there were in college. That was kind of different. Matter of fact, my grades did go down that year, from going back and forth to Detroit. I don't want to say we were refined, but . . . we learned a lot from Motown, too, in terms of being out on the road. Because we were around all sorts of people, at the theaters where we performed, we learned a lot, not so much the streets, but the gutbucket— how do you say it in a nice way?—well, we learned a lot about life.

As a teacher, that was probably one of the best things I could have done, to be a better teacher. I have to come in contact with all kinds of kids. What better preparation, than to go out on the road.

—Mildred Gill Arbor—

We started traveling and touring and singing at little sock hops, although we only could do it on the weekends. Bertha and I were the senior members of the group. I was out of high school, going to Western, then I started working that following year. I worked at McLaren Hospital in Flint, in the operating room, as an operating room technician.

I basically had just weekends off at work—it was just a lot of runnin' back and forth. I flunked out of Western, then I got married and had a couple of kids. And I can remember taking my two smaller kids to rehearsal down in Detroit, at the studio [then, pre-West Grand Blvd., it was located at Gordy family headquarters] at Farnsworth and St. Antoine. And I told my daughter this years later: Marvin Gaye changed her diapers!

I worked at McLaren Hospital for twelve years, then I filed for divorce. After that, I went back to school, in nursing. I went to school during the day, while my kids were in school, then I worked third shift, at night. I sort of slept in between.

—Carolyn "Cal" Gill Street—

We had to go to Detroit every other weekend to record. And then once we recorded, it was just a matter of time before they released a song.

The markets were limited and initially they would focus on local, state, and regional markets for our music. Then they would branch out later to the national market. The powers-that-be would decide what markets they'd put you out to.

And for the Velvelettes, it was more regional, initially, with our first song especially, "There He Goes," which we wrote, but we didn't get credit for, because we didn't know all the specifics of what it meant to claim ownership to a song.

Unbeknownst to us, Mickey Stevenson took credit for "There He Goes." Norma wrote it, and then we all collaborated and put the background in. But we didn't get credit for it because Mickey Stevenson took it and re-recorded it. Next thing we know, it was released with him being claimed as the writer. And it never got corrected.

I did the lead part on all the songs. We would do record hops on the weekend. Norma was in junior college, Bertha and Millie were in Western, [and] Betty Kelley and myself were still in high school. I went to Loy Norrix in Kalamazoo, and Betty Kelley went to Central. I was one of the first blacks to integrate my school; it made *Life* magazine at the time. They came to the churches and asked some of the pastors at the churches to integrate the schools. Well, my father volunteered me.

It was real tough, because there wasn't a day at school that I wasn't called the "n" word or harassed, not by the whole student population, but a pocket of ten or twelve who were just about the business of harassing all the minorities who came to the school. I was not happy, so singing in the Velvelettes was my outlet.

I couldn't wait for the weekend, because that would give me release from all that. I would either be in Detroit or rehearsing up at Western with the group. So I really didn't have friends my age. After a couple years of singing on the weekend, rehearsing with the group and all, it was time for me to make a move to the Detroit area. My aunt [Elzora] and uncle [Ezra], my father's brother, were childless, so I ended up moving to Detroit and living with them, on LaSalle at Pilgrim. I finished my senior year of high school there, at Chadsey High. Because we were doing record hops, we had to promote the records when they were released. And some of the records were released when I was in high school. "There He Goes" was.

And then, when I was a senior at Chadsey, we released "Needle In A Haystack." That song took off, and it became more than we could handle on the weekends, and we had to start promoting it. Berry promised my parents that they'd wait 'til high school graduation before they sent me out on the road, which they did; they waited.

But I had to do local Detroit record hops; Warren, Walled Lake, Canada for Robin Seymour's [Windsor-based TV show] *Swingin' Time*. They'd have a driver pick us up and take us to these places. But it got to be a bit much, and as time went on it was quite obvious that I was going to start traveling. Two weeks after I graduated, I was out on the road with the *Dick Clark Caravan of Stars*. We had to go to Chicago, meet up with the *Dick Clark Caravan*, and we were gone for six to eight weeks.

—Bertha Barbee McNeal—

I was in awe of the other Motown groups. These people like Stevie Wonder would walk through the studio, and we were happy to be there. I don't know if it's because we were from out of town, but we put them up on a pedestal. We were definitely in awe of Marvin Gaye. Not only that, he was handsome, but we loved the way he sang, too. One time he was sitting there, and he changed Mildred's baby's dydies. We were in the studio at the same time.

Martha and the Vandellas we were close to, probably because Betty Kelley joined them. That I have to say about the Velvelettes; we got along pretty good with the people on the shows. Berry had this whole thing where you felt like working for Motown was a family thing.

I don't know if it was because he came from a large family, but you'd see his mother and father walking around, fixing stuff. His father would always have a hammer in one hand— they were renovating those houses [the "Hitsville" house and adjacent ones used for offices on West Grand Boulevard] when we first came along, in the early sixties. Well, he was just as nice and down to earth as can be. So Berry came from a family, and he had those skills of making us feel that we were part of a family. It was the type of feeling where you would do anything for him. He made you feel good. So I'm going to put out the best of whatever this talent is. They had a knack of doing that.

In the summer, they'd have picnics for all of us. You'd bring your family, and he would supply the food. They'd have parties, big, splashy Christmas parties. He'd give gifts to all the groups; he'd have some groups sing. The Velvelettes one year got crystal jewelry—a necklace and earrings—and I still have that. I remember one year Diana Ross and the Supremes were doing their number one tunes, and he gave them diamonds! So you'd love to hear your name. He'd call your names out to come up and get your gifts, as a group. He had a way of making you feel a part of things.

They also had what they called the "Battle of the Stars" [at the Graystone Ballroom, a Woodward Avenue jazz ballroom from the '20s, purchased by Gordy]. Believe it or not, the Velvelettes beat out the Supremes a few times. This was before they had their big hits; they just had their first couple of tunes. The audience would have to clap; that's how they'd run the battle. The Temptations would go against the Miracles, or the Marvelettes against Martha and the Vandellas. Still, even then it wasn't a rivalry thing. It was a show that the kids were getting, but it was making it fun.

Fun it might have been, but Diana Ross didn't take losing to the Velvelettes very gracefully.

—Norma Barbee Fairhurst—

Diane had to go to the bathroom, and unfortunately for her, I had to go at the same time. She was kicking the door and screaming and just having a fit that we'd won. And it was no big deal to us!

As a music major, Bertha Barbee McNeal was especially excited to work with Motown's legendary Funk Brothers.

—Bertha Barbee McNeal—

Me being a piano player, Earl Van Dyke was my idol! We met Earl Van Dyke first, when he played for the Barbees. Norma and I figured that out when we finally cut our first Motown record, "There He Goes," which Norma wrote. We were going, "He's the piano player who played for us before!"

He could sit down at that piano, and if you were singing something, and it was a little too high, or a little too low, this man could transpose like nobody's business! His technique, his rhythm, what he could do with those chords, I'm telling you.

A curator from the Henry Ford Museum was lucky enough to find Earl Van Dyke's own Hammond B-3 organ, broken down and gathering dust in a music store in Detroit—at least, the store owner claimed it was Earl's. The curator bought it and it's now in the Motown Museum.

You know how Princess Diana auctioned off her dresses? Anything that belonged to Earl Van Dyke, I'd be down there with my life savings to buy it.

Those three, the bassist, the piano player, and the drummer [James Jamerson, Van Dyke, and Benny Benjamin, respectively], they were the core of what you called the Motown sound.

You had that little bit of jazz, with this rock thing coming in, and they mixed that. And I'm sure they had the background of being in church, gospel. Someone stirred it all together, and out came this Motown sound.

Our harmony was our strongest asset. That's how we got the name the Velvelettes. We all had the ability, when we got together as kids, one person would sing a note, and the others would harmonize. We could do four-part harmony. Our first name was Les Jolies Femmes, then one day in the car we were harmonizing, coming up with all these different sounds. Finally somebody said, "That sounds as smooth as velvet."

The Velvelettes may have had some polish from their years of schooling, but being a Motown diva was something else entirely. They were put through what, by the mid-sixties, was the standard Motown finishing school process, including Maxine Powell's famous etiquette classes.

—Carolyn "Cal" Gill Street—

Mrs. Powell came on the scene when they were preparing us to go out. She had been working with the Supremes and the Vandellas and the Marvelettes. So we were the last group to come on board. The Gordys knew her way before that. We had to take artist development classes. Later on, they brought in Cholly Atkins, the choreographer. Mrs. Powell was the finishing school teacher, and Maurice King and Harvey Fuqua were the vocal coaches. It took place in an artist development facility over on St. Antoine and Farnsworth.

It was mandatory that you go there when you weren't working and weren't on the road. Because that's where you learned all your skills and stage presentation; how to execute a song, how to "sell" a song. Routines, vocals, all that stuff.

The artist development facility was in one of the Gordy properties in their old neighborhood, in and around the corner of St. Antoine and Farnsworth.

They had converted some of the rooms downstairs. It was like an apartment building. Their printing business was in it. And a few of the rooms were converted to studios; all the walls were mirrored, to watch yourself when you were learning choreography, and they had a big grand piano. It was for the artists. You were scheduled to go over there when you were in town and not working. It was an ongoing process that you went through. You were critiqued.

The Velvelettes were among those artists left behind when Motown moved west in the early 1970s (it was a rolling move, with the final push in 1972).

—Bertha Barbee McNeal—

It wasn't the best feeling in the world. It was like, "Well, shoot!" To be honest, I thought it was going to be the end of the Motown era. I don't think it ended there; Motown will never end, as far as that goes. I wasn't too happy to see that, it was like "Detroit, Motown"—it all went together. That was their home.

What happened was, afterwards we did tours—*Shindig*, Dick Clark tours, and all that. We were at the marrying age, as we called it, so we opted to get married and start families anyway. Cal decided to keep the group going. Before we left to start our families, we made sure there were girls to take our places. Because Cal thought she'd sing for a year or two before she got married. So when Motown went west, we weren't under contract. We were starting our families.

But performing is in your blood. You become addicted to it. I would be changing diapers, and see girls performing, and in the back of my mind, I'm going, "*Oooo*, I really like doing that." So it never really leaves you, the love of doing it.

—*Carolyn "Cal" Gill Street*—

I finally decided I was going back to school in the early seventies to prepare myself for some alternative employment, 'cause this was not going to last forever . . . it became clearer and clearer to me as time went on that in order to maintain that level of success where you could live comfortably and maintain a certain lifestyle, you had to be totally dedicated to the profession, to the business. It required a lot of sacrifice, more than I was willing to give. We looked at it as a good time. It was more fun and exciting to go to all these places, to get on a plane and go to New York and L.A. and Chicago—it was more exciting to do that than even to make money. Because we were young! So our focus wasn't on making the money.

Unfortunately, we spent a lot! We just had a ball! Flying in and out, shopping trips to New York, when we were off. It was like more fun in our lives than anything.

Once we all got married, the group was reduced to four in the late sixties because Betty Kelley joined the Vandellas. "Dancing In The Street" was a smash, and they were committed to go to England to perform. But one lady in the Vandellas, Annette, because of spousal pressures, couldn't go. Her husband told her she couldn't go. The company was committed to the contracts and had to have somebody take her place. Because I was still in high school and we weren't really traveling out of Detroit anyway, they asked Betty Kelley to go to England [with the Vandellas]. Betty was the same height, color, size, everything, as Annette. All they had to do was just slide her in. They didn't have to explain anything to the tour people in England; she was a perfect match.

After that, Betty joined the Vandellas, with our blessing. We thought it was a great opportunity for her, and there was no sense in her waiting around for me to get out of high school to make some money on her own.

And you know, her voice was already on "Dancing In The Street." Because Motown was in the habit of using whatever artists were available, whenever they wanted to add meat to a song, especially the background, they would ask whatever artists were available around the studio, or they'd call your house and say, "Are you available to do this session? We need more voices." So Betty sang on "Dancing In The Street," and her voice is quite clear on that master, in the background. She ended up signing a contract because the other girl's husband was not going to let her go back with the Vandellas anytime soon.

So we were reduced to four. And not long after Kelley left for the Vandellas, the Velvelettes went into disarray. We still managed to do some gigs together, but it came to a time where Bertha's husband pressured her to stop. And Mildred's husband pressured her to stop. Then Norma got married. So I'm left holding the ball and having to keep the group together because we had contracts signed for us to perform. So I auditioned several ladies. One of them came from New York, one from Ohio, two or three from Detroit, for replacements for the Velvelettes. I selected two, and they went on to do several shows with me for a year or two.

But then it got to the point where I thought, I'll put this on the back burner for a while. And I married Richard Street. At that time, he was a Monitor, but he was becoming a member of the Temptations, because Paul Williams was getting sick. Once I married him—the Temptations were very popular then—I really didn't have to work. I'd gone back to school, Detroit Business College, and the Detroit Institute of Commerce, trying to get some skills so I could work a straight gig. And I'd gotten a job at Ford Motor Company—I worked at Ford Tractor Division in Birmingham, then I ended up back in the "Glass House" [Ford headquarters in Dearborn] before I quit, when I was five months pregnant with my son.

I became a homemaker and housewife, since Richard was making all this money with the Temptations.

The Velvelettes never left mid-Michigan, so perhaps it's inevitable that they would get back together in 1984, despite the marriages, the children, and the careers.

—Bertha Barbee McNeal—

A group here in Kalamazoo, Black Concerned Women

of Kalamazoo, they were giving a conference, and they were going to feature African-American women. I was chairman of the music committee. We were going to get someone to sing like famous singers of each decade.

So we got to the sixties, and someone said, "Bertha, weren't you in a group? We could get your group to represent the sixties." I was going, "Get out of here. There's no way." Our kids were still in school. But I made the phone call to the girls, and they said, "Get out of here!" But we said, "Let's do it, just one time." We thought we'd get a medley together of girl group songs, like "Maybe" by the Shirelles, "We Are Family" by Sister Sledge. So we got together at Cal's brother's house, and the old feelings started coming back. We were at the piano, and got our medley together. Got our hair fixed up, and our mothers all came.

We sang our medley, and the ladies in that audience went bananas. We were thinking, if these people became this excited for us . . . So we said, "Shoot, we like the feeling we got onstage." Especially at the age we were, we were more appreciative. We were actually making people feel good, and that was a good feeling. It's weird because next thing we knew, somebody called and said, "Would you guys sing at the Fox Theatre? Martha and the Vandellas, Mary Wells . . . " You can imagine, for us to be on that show. And it just snowballed from there.

But will the Midwest-bound Velvelettes ever gain any measure of respect?

—Mildred Gill Arbor—

The Rock and Roll Hall of Fame hasn't inducted us yet, and I doubt that they ever will! There are people out there for whom this has been their life. It has not been our lives, it's been a part of it. We've excelled at other endeavors.

When we originally started, it was like, "This is going to be really fun!" But the older you get, I hated it, hated it, hated it. Now that we do things, it isn't that stressful, because you get to choose where you go, who you do it with. We try to do things on the weekend.

—Carolyn "Cal" Gill Street—

Our contributions to the industry, like "Needle In A Haystack," "(He Was) Really Saying Something," "These Things Will Keep Me Loving You," those things have kept our name out there.

Just as there are "fake" Marvelettes, there are some faux Velvelettes on the concert circuit.

—Carolyn "Cal" Gill Street—

In England there was a group that spelled the name "Velvellettes." We don't know where they were from, but they credited themselves with having done our songs. We saw pictures of them when we were over in England. Could not believe it! Could not believe it!

You can't really police and monitor that. Over in Europe the laws are so different, even with copyrights. After 25 years of something being out there, it's in the public domain. And you can't claim it after that time. Whereby in the States, it's different. You're always the owner of that product.

Ultimately, the Velvelettes were in the same spot as all female groups at Motown: the Supremes truly were Supreme.

—Norma Barbee Fairhurst—

It was pretty obvious that Berry was going to advance who he was going to advance. I can only speak for myself, but I compare this with other corporations. In your job, did you ever find other people being advanced over you, and you were just as smart, and you said, "Well, why?" That was like Diane; he was promoting her over the other ladies. And I think we all felt the same way—the Marvelettes and Martha Reeves. We talked about it. The Supremes had the better wardrobe, the better everything, even the better Christmas gifts! We asked about that, and they said, "Well, it's because they've had more hits." It's like a family, and one daughter gets a better dress than the other daughter. We certainly looked at these things, but then we'd say, "Oh well, what the heck." But he promoted who he wanted to . . . and it's obvious, as the years go by, why. They had a love affair going.

The men probably didn't give a hoot, but you know how we are as women.

We had a homecoming with Mrs. Edwards, Berry's sister [Motown museum founder Esther Gordy Edwards] about 15 years ago. We took her to dinner and reformed that friendship, and it was wonderful. We went back to her apartment and talked, and one of the things she mentioned, she said, "You know, I told my brother to promote the Velvelettes, to do more with them, but he said, 'No, I don't want those attorneys on my back.'"

This actually came from her mouth. I'm sure you know what he was talking about, the attorneys our folks had when we signed the [Motown] contract, because we were too young. And they wouldn't let our attorneys through the door. Would not let them look at the contract.

Well, I cried and cried until my parents signed anyway. What he was talking about, well, Berry didn't want to have those lawyers on his back. He didn't want to have to account to anybody.

Chapter Eleven
—Tammi Terrell—

TAMMI TERRELL WASN'T QUITE 25 when she died of
a brain tumor in 1970, but something about the way her
effervescent voice blended with Marvin Gaye's languid tenor
has kept their duets alive, as compelling as when they were
recorded in the sixties.

She was born Thomasina Montgomery in Philadelphia
on January 24, 1946, and called "Tommy" by her friends
and family. The Montgomerys lived in the picturesque
Germantown section of Philadelphia, and the outgoing,
vivacious Tammi had a shy younger sister, Ludie. The
family often spent summers at the Jersey shore, and Tammi
won a contest in New Jersey when she was just eleven. She
was playing theaters and clubs in Pennsylvania and New
Jersey by the time she was thirteen. Fellow Philadelphian
Lynda Laurence, later of the Supremes, recalls seeing
Tammi perform at the Beachcomber Club in the shore
town of Wildwood, N.J., along with Gary U.S. Bonds, Patti
LaBelle and the Blue Belles, and Bunny Sigler.

There are several persistent Tammi rumors. One was

*that she was married to boxer Ernie Terrell. Terrell was the
brother of Jean Terrell of the Supremes, but no husband to
Tammi, who'd simply adopted "Terrell" as a shorter, more
marquee-friendly name than "Montgomery."*

*Tammi signed with Scepter/Wand when she was
fourteen and performed live with top performers of the day
such as Jerry Butler, and several years later, the James Brown
Revue. Romantic relationships with Brown and later, David
Ruffin of the Temptations, were reportedly marked with abuse.*

*In the late sixties, when her blinding headaches led to the
diagnosis of a brain tumor, friends made the association between the feisty Terrell's physical tussles with those boyfriends
and her illness.*

*Although her doctors discounted the connection, the
stories persisted, and because the source of the stories was
often her fellow Motown artists, the narrative was persistent.*

*What we do know is that she signed with Motown in 1965,
and after several years of lukewarm solo releases, she was
paired with Gaye. Their duets, as produced by Nick Ashford
and Valerie Simpson—songs like "Ain't No Mountain High
Enough," "You're All I Need (To Get By)," and "Your Precious
Love"—stand as a stunning accomplishment.*

*According to her sister, Ludie Montgomery, Tammi was
very sick for the last two years of her life and underwent eight
operations. She finally came home to Philadelphia, where her
sister would hold her in her arms as she became weaker and
eventually lost her sight. Her death was such a blow to her
family that they remember her exact time of death on that
March day: 8:55 a.m.*

In his live concerts during the years before his death in 1984, Gaye would often call for the audience to applaud for Terrell.

"Go ahead," he'd say. "She can hear you."

—Martha Reeves—

I knew Tammi, I was making my decision to leave Motown when Tammi arrived. And at first I kind of envied Tammi because she was doing what I wanted to do, sing with Marvin Gaye. We'd sing backup for Marvin, but I never actually sang a duet with him, and I always wanted to do that. And I felt the songs that they gave Tammi, I could have done a very good job on, too. The same writers that had favored me for a long time started favoring her. But it made me see how Motown operated: they would make an artist, then move on to the next one.

Tammi Terrell at the height of her fame at Motown, when she and duet partner Marvin Gaye were everybody's dream sweethearts.

—Elaine Jesmer—

Tammi taught me how to fight. She taught this white girl how to fight. I said, "I have to fight?" She said, "You do if you want to get out of this alley." We were in Chicago and some girl gang showed up. She kind of cooked it, but said, "Look, just do what I tell you to do. If anybody comes close, you hit them." Yeah, but she was fierce. A wonderful, fierce person. She died young because she burned out young; she had to. If you look at the tapes of her and Marvin singing together, you can see it; she loved the idea that she could kick Marvin's ass.

He didn't want to deal with her. But her attitude was, "You know, you're gonna deal with me." It was a wonderful relationship—I think he thought he'd have forever to work it out. He thought he'd get a chance. But she would have had to get him into bed. It would never be him to get her into bed. They goaded each other, so it could have happened. But it wasn't something that defined their relationship.

Physical violence was not a foreign thing to her or to any of those guys. Oh yeah, she was so proud that she hit [David Ruffin] with a lamp. She was fearless and fiendish . . . she was way ahead of us all.

—Brenda Holloway—

Tammi was my best friend at Motown. We would go out when she was in L.A. We spent a lot of time together. And when she really got sick, that really devastated me. Her motor skills were gone, and she would just have shopping bags full of medications. And it would do something to me. At that time Jimi Hendrix overdosed, then Mama Cass [from The Mamas and the Papas]—all these people were leaving. You were about peace and love and happiness, and you see all these people dying like flies.

Tammi was very troubled, because she was Tammi Montgomery and she was with James Brown, before. She was probably physically sick before she came to Motown and didn't know it. Then with the arguments and the fights that she and David Ruffin had, it just aggravated, I think, a previous injury, and then it just got out of hand and I guess it became malignant, a brain tumor.

She was a very, very sad, sad little person who was looking for love, and she paid the price for the love she didn't have. She was a beautiful woman but she was looking for love and she was willing to pay a price. Maybe she felt guilty because of her looks. They feel guilty because they can get anyone they want. But once you get them, is this what you really want? After you find out about the person you've attracted, you can't shake loose. And she just got attached to the wrong people. She was vulnerable because her heart was exposed. Like Marilyn [Monroe], she exposed her heart too much. You have to be careful, going into a relationship, you can't expose your heart too much.

She was the aggressor [toward Marvin]. Marvin was unpredictable. Marvin had a split personality. Offstage he was an introvert, in his shell, and he was an extrovert onstage. He was comfortable onstage, and very troubled offstage. So I did not like to be around him offstage. But I *loooved* to be in his arms onstage. Yes!

He was a troubled man. He was searching for Marvin. He was, again, beautiful, but very, very insecure. Tammi had to be insecure because of what she was willing to go through. There are a lot of insecure people in the world.

—Carolyn "Cal" Gill Street—

I didn't know her deeply, but I'd been over to her house when she and David Ruffin lived together. I had more involved experiences with some of the other artists [than the other Velvelettes] because I was on the scene, I lived in Detroit. I think it was off Chicago Boulevard.

Tammi was a nice lady . . . the best I could say, in working with her on different shows, she was an excellent artist and performer, but she seemed to be troubled.

—Kim Weston—

I knew Tammi when she was Tammi Montgomery. She played with Chuck Jackson at the 20 Grand a couple of times. And she'd come around when we played the Uptown in Philly.

There was a rumor out that many artists were told not to talk to us [Weston and her husband, Mickey Stevenson], after we left Motown. A few of them did walk by me, which hurt me, although I got over it. But after I got over the initial hurt, then I'd run into them, and it would still hurt. You can't live with people, eat and sleep with them, without having some type of feelings. Those feelings don't disappear just because somebody tells you don't. I know some of them were probably intimidated by administrative things.

As a matter of fact, it was Tammi Terrell who was the one who called me and told me what was said. Her remark was, "Can't no so-and-so tell me I can't talk to you. I knew you before I knew them!" Those were her famous words to me. She was quite a lady.

—*Mickey Stevenson*—

I loved Tammi Terrell; she was great. She was streetwise. What made us an unusual marriage, with these ladies over there, was the streetwise ladies would inform some of the ones that were not, to beware. Which helped them quite a bit. And the ones that were not, would inform some of the streetwise ladies how to have a bit more class. We had a training class, we took on Maxine Powell to work with our ladies and give 'em something, so when we brought in people from outside to join our company, we offered them the opportunity to do that. But when they watched these ladies develop with a lot of style and class, even though they wouldn't take the classes, they would take from the [other] girls. So it kind of worked itself out.

But Tammi was a streetwise girl; she got that from New York. You do that or get killed. She could definitely handle herself. And with that, she never had to get into it with any-body. Here in Detroit, we're all trying to be somebody. There was a funny line, "Who do you think you are, you trying to be somebody?" I'd say, "Absolutely yes. And any of your boyfriends don't understand that, pass them on, you don't need to be bothered with that individual."

Knowing Tammi and knowing men, I know that it's very possible that she was involved in abusive situations. I didn't assume it wasn't true; I just tried to help her out the best I could. Women don't always make the best choices in this business with their relationships. I don't know why it's that way, it's just uncanny. Black or white. Either somebody doesn't want to be Mr. Terrell or Mr. Ross; therefore the guys may come on with one thing, but down the line they make it very difficult. By this time, love has set its course, and they can't seem to get out of it, the women. Takes them a hard time to get out of relationships. We had to resolve a few of them ourselves, at Motown.

To this day, at my age, I still don't understand it. Most of them [at Motown] had this kind of problem. The only ones who didn't were the ones who were totally dedicated to their careers. They were the ones who took on relationships only as a fulfillment of a need, not a demand for a living. Their lives were the art itself. In Diana Ross' case, and a few others.

—Katherine Anderson Schaffner—

Very strong singing ability. I got to know Tammi long before she came to Motown, when she was working out on the road on different shows that we had done, as Tammi Montgomery. She had terrific singing ability. She was, like Mary Wells, very sweet. And all of us, I would have to say, were very naive. Naive about men, *mmm-hmm*.

SUSAN WHITALL is a former editor of *Creem Magazine*, and longtime music writer for *The Detroit News*. She is also the author of *Fever: Little Willie John's Fast Life, Mysterious Death, and the Birth of Soul*, and the forthcoming *Joni Mitchell on Joni Mitchell: Interviews and Encounters*.

Other Books in
the Great Music Book Series

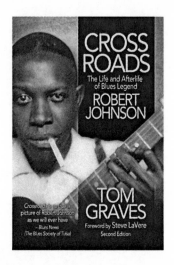

*Crossroads: The Life and Afterlife of Blues Legend
Robert Johnson*
by Tom Graves

This second edition of the award-winning *Crossroads*
by Tom Graves is the author-approved new manuscript that
contains updated information and new photographs related to
blues legend Robert Johnson. *Crossroads* won the Keeping
the Blues Alive Award in Literature in 2010 from the pres-
tigious Blues Foundation and is considered the definitive
word on its enigmatic subject.

The result of careful and meticulous research, this
stylishly-written biography of infamous blues musician
Robert Johnson reveals the real story behind the mythical
talent that made him a musical legend. Available in print,
ebook, and audiobook, read by the author himself.

Sun Records: An Oral History
by John Floyd

Rock 'n' roll was created in tiny Sun Records in Memphis, Tennessee, by owner Sam Phillips, who introduced the world to Elvis, Johnny Cash, Jerry Lee Lewis, Rufus Thomas, Carl Perkins, and many others.

Brush up on your knowledge of Sun's legendary performers by purchasing a copy of *Sun Records: An Oral History* from Devault-Graves Digital Editions.

You'll be treated to the voices of the pillars of Sun, the artists, producers and engineers who made the place tick. *Sun Records: An Oral History* by author John Floyd is available in print and ebook formats.

That's All Right, Mama
by Gerald Duff

Did Elvis' identical twin, Jesse Garon Presley, really die at birth?

Not according to Lance Lee, the hero of Gerald Duff's darkly comic dissection of fame and rock 'n' roll.

Lee, who makes his living as an Elvis imitator, claims to be the long-presumed dead twin. In a style that faithfully reproduces Elvis' plaintive bravado, Lance-Jesse recounts being hidden away and passed off as Elvis' "cousin" until he needs to impersonate Elvis to stave off bullies at school; later, he is obliged to "play Elvis" every time The King has an attack of nerves.

As performing substitute, Jesse has had a lifetime to enjoy being a good-timing, honey-loving, non-drug-dependent Elvis.

CPSIA information can be obtained
at www.ICGtesting.com
Printed in the USA
LVOW07s1911211117
557189LV00004B/735/P